Build Wealth *in any* Market

How to create consistent, reliable income from the stock market

Ross W. Jardine

Marketplace Books
Columbia, Maryland

Publisher: Chris Myers
VP/General Manager: John Boyer
Development Editor: Jody Costa
Art Director: Larry Strauss
Interior Design & Production: Jennifer Marin
Production Coordinator: Angela Collins

ISBN: 1-59280-334-2
ISBN 13: 978-1-59280-334-7
Printed in the United States of America.

The educated investor must acknowledge that there are bull and bear markets and they must learn the skills to take advantage of both types of market behavior

—ROSS JARDINE

TABLE OF CONTENTS

PREFACE

For over a decade, I've traveled the world teaching thousands of individual investors how to survive and prosper in our volatile stock markets. Through all that experience, I've come to a simple conclusion: the single biggest challenge almost all investors face is that they universally lose money unless stocks are rising. Most investors make money when stocks are rising as long as they are invested in something. In a bull market, making money is easy for most investors. Some will make more than others based upon their individual stock selection, but most make money.

If individual investors have learned anything over the past decade or so, it's that markets don't always go up. In fact, we've recently experienced one of the most devastating bear markets in history as well as several other pretty good sized dips that have dramatically impacted the value of most every investor's account.

From the time I was a little boy until my college days, I wanted to be a professional baseball player. I loved all sports, but baseball was my passion. As an athlete, you constantly train to improve your performance. In nearly any sport, the best way to improve your overall performance is to focus your practice on your weakest skills. If you can't seem to hit a curve ball, you get some extra batting practice with lots of curve balls. If you're making too many fielding errors, you take extra ground balls to improve your fielding.

I like to apply the same simple logic to investing. If individual investors want to be better overall investors and make more money, more consistently in any kind of market conditions, then they need to focus more time on improving in the areas where they are weakest. That area is making money when stocks are NOT rising.

I love to teach people about investing. It's my profession and my passion. In my 20 years of investing my own money, I've learned there are a number of strategies I could use to protect myself and prosper when stocks are flat or falling. The strategies are not hard and virtually any investor could learn how to apply them. That was my motivation for writing this book. I want to share with you some of the simple strategies and concepts that you can use to preserve your precious trading capital when the market drops and find opportunities to actually make money when nearly every other individual investor is suffering losses.

Asset allocation and diversity will not protect you when all stocks are falling, as is the case in nearly every bear market. It's time to think differently about investing and to stop losing money when the market drops. It's time you learned the strategies that you can use to protect yourself from falling stock prices, and ways to even profit from it.

Many investors always seem to have one or two catastrophic investments each year. These are the ones that they played a little bigger because they were sure they would make a bundle. But what happened instead? The bottom fell out of their stock unexpectedly, and they ended up losing most or all of their money on that trade.

When I teach live classes, I often ask the students to think back to the last catastrophic investment they made and try to remember exactly how much money they lost. It's not a pleasant memory, but most remember the amount to the penny. I then ask them if they had not lost that amount on that one single disastrous trade, would it have improved their overall performance for the entire year by one, two, or three percent? Most nod their heads in agreement.

The way I see it, they could eliminate one bad decision each year and improve their overall performance by one to three percent. That's some pretty easy money. Think about the impact of compounding that additional money over a lifetime of investing, and I think you'd agree that it could amount to a ton of extra money for retirement or lifestyle enhancements. Well, the good news is that there are some very simple things that you can do to totally eliminate those catastrophic investments that seem to sink your results year after year, and I'm going to share them with you in this book. If after reading this book and applying some of these simple strategies you ever have another catastrophic investment, all I have to say is "Shame on you."

I recently attended a large investment conference put on by a big brokerage firm. In the presentation by their chief investment strategist, they told the audience that it was impossible to time the market and that they would be better off just staying invested in a widely diversified portfolio to ride out the dips. To illustrate the negative impact of trying to time the market they showed a slide that revealed the impact of missing out on the 10 biggest trading days of the year. It was quite an impact.

I don't want you to get the impression that I'm trying to teach you how to time the market. My focus in this book is to teach you good investment management. Few brokers will ever tell you to go to cash, but in a bear market the interest on a money market account usually outperforms every other investment class. I agree we all need the benefit of being invested on all of the best days in the market to get the maximum results, but imagine if you could eliminate some or all of the 10 worst trading days each year. I think you'd do better overall than just staying invested all the time and doing nothing. That's the potential of the concepts you'll learn in this book.

Let's look at current conditions. Since the last bear market ended in 2003, the market has gone straight up for nearly five straight years. From the market low in September of 2002 to the recent highs near the end of 2007, the market has recovered 80 percent, proving once again that powerful bull markets often follow bear markets. I'm writing this book at the start of 2008 and many of the market conditions that preceded the last bear market are starting to appear again. Speculation is high, and many fortunes have been made in the past five years. Real estate prices have also exploded, and many people have tapped the equity in their home to capitalize on it.

Certainly, some of that money has found its way into the stock market, helping to fuel the current rally. When money becomes plentiful and investors seem willing to buy into any story regardless of the economic underpinnings, it's a clear sign we're closer to the top than the bottom.

Those investors who were brave enough to get back in the market at the end of the last bear market have been richly rewarded. Unfortunately, many investors suffered catastrophic losses during the last bear market and either had no money left to invest or simply didn't have the nerves to get back in the market again.

Any investors who have been in the market during the past decade have had the opportunity to experience a full market cycle from exorbitant highs to devastating lows. The slow and steady returns that nearly every financial planner and broker bases their projections on seem to be a thing of the past. The current generation of investors have had to deal with dramatic swings in the market that create huge fluctuations in their account values and equally challenging swings in their individual emotions.

The "buy and hold" approach that most have used their entire investing lives is starting to show signs of vulnerability. It's true that the market goes up a lot more than it goes down; but, if you were one of the unlucky ones to endure one of the recent bear markets, you may not have had much growth at all, even if you had a well-diversified portfolio that you held for the long haul.

Many investors nearing retirement were already upgrading their plans to spend the profits they had earned during the great bull market of the late 90's. After suffering catastrophic losses in their portfolios during the bear market, many are now forced to scale back on those plans or even put off retirement altogether and keep working just to maintain the quality of life they currently enjoy.

When I talk to investors who suffered great losses during the last bear market, I ask them if they ever had a plan to sell at some price. Few did. Rather than put the safety net up, they trusted a broker to let them know when it was time to sell or relied on their gut to tell them it was time. Neither worked. What took years to make was lost in a matter of months.

If recent history has taught us anything, it's that every investor needs to prepare for the next bear market or serious correction while times are good, because if they wait, thinking they will recognize the change when it comes, it will be too late. The time to prepare your portfolio for the next bear market is not when stocks have already begun falling, but while they are setting new highs.

The focus of this book is on teaching you how to recognize when the trend of the market is changing and give you a wide range of strategies to apply in flat and down markets to continue to profit, or at a minimum, stop losing so much money. It rips my heart out when I hear the stories of investors who were nearing retirement back in the late 90's who were not prepared for the devastating bear market that struck in 2000 and ended up losing so much of their nest egg.

If you lost 40, 50, 60 percent or more of your portfolio value in the last bear market, this book will be one of the best investments you'll ever make. Many of the strategies you'll learn in this book with very slight modifications can be used in any kind of market conditions to protect you and help you find profit opportunities.

Many of the strategies you'll learn in this book are what I like to call "income strategies." These strategies are designed to help you learn how to generate consistent and reliable income from your investments in the stock market. The strategies are simple to learn and very conservative, so they work for nearly any investor. I don't know about you, but I hate losing trades. One of the benefits of using my income strategies is that they tend to have a higher probability of success in a wide variety of market conditions. I like that.

If you've never made money when stocks are flat or falling, this book will open your eyes to a whole new world of investment opportunities. The days of sitting and watching your account fall when stocks decline will be a thing of the past if you can just master a few of the simple strategies in this book.

And, the strategies I teach in this book are simple. Anyone can learn them and employ them in a matter of days. But, they will only protect you if you use them.

I've spent the better part of my career striving to help investors learn to navigate the markets. In 2003, I chose to retire from Investools to take a break from all the travel and instead spend more time at home with my wonderful family and pursue some other interests. Over the five years from the time my partner and I started our company, we built one of the leaders in investor education, and I had the opportunity to teach and train thousands of investors all over the world. It was a great experience and something that makes me immensely proud.

After a couple years away from the industry, I realized I still had a great passion for teaching and training. In 2005, I started a new company, along with my former partners, to bring my powerful and simple approach to investing to the masses of investors who are searching for direction. My primary focus with this new business is to make quality investor education and powerful tools and training available to every investor at a reasonable price. It's been a great success, and I invite you to check out Stockinvestor.com to learn more about our powerful tools and training.

Ross Jardine

Founder, Stock Investor

INTRODUCTION

The year 2000 was very memorable, especially for anyone attempting to navigate the stock market. As the year began, most of us were poised and waiting for the millennium bug to crash computers all over the world and precipitate a financial meltdown.

Instead, as the markets turned bearish and stock prices collapsed, many investors felt the financial meltdown as they witnessed many of the gains made over the past few years wiped out in a matter of months. This was easily one of the most volatile periods in the history of the stock market.

The explosive growth of the Internet and a raging bull market has brought millions of new investors into the market over the past decade. Investors grew accustomed to 20+ percent returns and lost sight of the fact that markets do not always go up. In fact, many investors borrowed heavily and poured every cent into the market, figuring an almost certain windfall would easily cover the interest.

But, the market changed so dramatically, many investors struggled with the fact that what worked so well for them during the past decade simply didn't work anymore. Unwilling to admit that things changed, many investors continued to apply their bullish strategies, only to find themselves digging an even deeper financial hole. Many became so afraid of losing more money that they simply pulled out of the market completely. Welcome to the bear market.

Markets never go up forever, and investors need to learn to recognize the major market trends and adjust their strategies accordingly. The natural tendency of most investors is to have a bullish bias, which is their single biggest weakness when the market turns bearish.

As we find ourselves faced with circumstances that are much more challenging, our need for knowledge becomes greater. This is one of the things that prompted the writing of this book, *Build Wealth in any Market: How to Create Consistent, Reliable Income from the Stock Market*, as it is exactly what investors need to weather the storm—a simple plan.

This book is simply an introduction to strategies for surviving, and even profiting, in an extremely volatile market. I am confident it will give you some of the tools and resources needed to restore your confidence in investing in the markets and allow you to take control of your portfolio. Most of all, I hope you learn something here that helps you to be better prepared for the next bear market. It's coming. I don't know when, but I do know if you're not prepared when it strikes, it will be too late and you will suffer great losses as a result.

Some of the things that I address in this book are slight variations of the strategies you would use during a bull market. My intent is to teach you how to succeed in this very challenging market, right now. Or, at the very least, to teach you how to protect yourself against catastrophic losses and help you preserve your capital.

Historically, bear markets do not last as long as bull markets, but they can leave an indelible imprint on the memories of those investors who have survived one. After a bear market, people never again look at investing in the stock market with the same level of confidence. Just as bear markets can be profitable to those applying the appropriate strategies, once the bear market ends, there are greater opportunities for those using the bullish investment techniques that they have learned or used in the past.

In the basic investing seminars that I have taught all over the world, I teach investors to use both technical analysis and fundamental analysis. Investors learn how to read charts and understand some of the most common technical indicators. I also introduce some basic strategies such as using covered calls to generate income and playing stock splits with options. Judging from the e-mails and feedback that I've received from the thousands of students who have taken my courses, I feel qualified to help you through these very difficult times.

The purpose of this book is to give you a few simple steps you can take to preserve your capital, or perhaps find some opportunity where most investors see none. I am going to help you understand exactly how to survive in volatile markets, and perhaps even find opportunities and profits—if you're willing to apply some simple bearish strategies.

First, let's look at the overall big picture of the market to get a visual point of reference of the impact of a bear market.

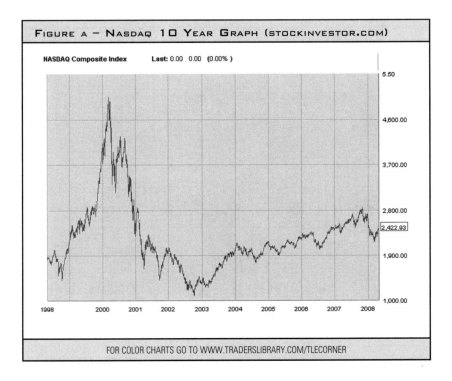

FIGURE A — NASDAQ 10 YEAR GRAPH (STOCKINVESTOR.COM)

NASDAQ Composite Index   Last: 0.00 0.00 (0.00%)

FOR COLOR CHARTS GO TO WWW.TRADERSLIBRARY.COM/TLECORNER

So what is a bear market anyway? I am sure that everyone has heard this term, but, by definition, what does it really mean? We associate bear markets with falling stock prices. If we look at the last 10 years, we can see that some very dramatic things took place in the market—particularly the NASDAQ market. The last bear market began in the first quarter of 2000 and lasted until near the end of 2002. While nearly every sector of the market was affected, technology stocks, the Internet stocks in particular, were the hardest hit.

By pulling up some of the numbers on the market, you can get a better idea of just how bad it was. Most experts will typically define a bear market as any decline in the major market index of 20 percent or more. Looking again at the last seven months of the year 2000, we saw almost a 50 percent decline in the NASDAQ market from the March highs (see Figure A). Many of the technology stocks that led us through the great bull market of the previous

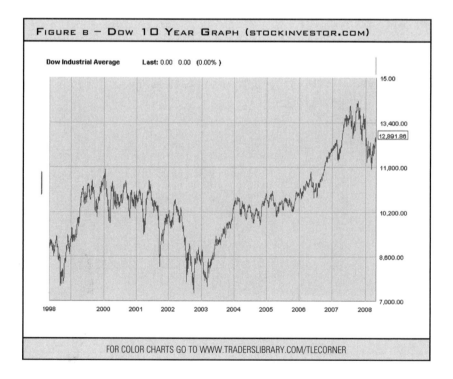

FIGURE B – DOW 10 YEAR GRAPH (STOCKINVESTOR.COM)

Dow Industrial Average   Last: 0.00 0.00 (0.00%)

FOR COLOR CHARTS GO TO WWW.TRADERSLIBRARY.COM/TLECORNER

seven years were trading at just a fraction of their highs from just seven months earlier.

Looking at some of the other major indexes, you can probably get a feel for what happened. In Figure B, the Dow Jones Industrial Average was down about 10 percent over the same period, a mere correction by normal standards.

The S&P 500 (Figure C) which is made up of a much broader group of stocks, was down about 16 percent. Obviously a lot of those fallen technology stocks have had a bearing on this index as well.

It's easy to see, by looking at any of these charts, that the markets were falling for much of the year 2000 and continued to fall for the next two years. The fact you are reading this book would indicate that you're concerned about losing money when the market falls. If you endured this bear market and felt its

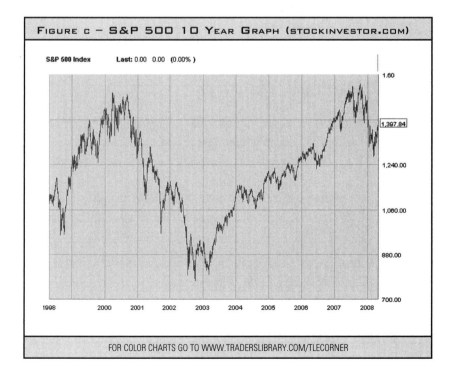

FIGURE C — S&P 500 10 YEAR GRAPH (STOCKINVESTOR.COM)

S&P 500 Index   Last: 0.00 0.00 (0.00%)

FOR COLOR CHARTS GO TO WWW.TRADERSLIBRARY.COM/TLECORNER

impact on your portfolio, it's not likely you'll soon forget it. If you're like most other investors, who've experienced a bear market, you felt angry, upset, and probably a little helpless and disappointed. And above it all, when it finally ended you were poorer than when it began.

No one likes losing money. It's one of my least favorite things. Unfortunately, during the last bear market, many investors experienced significant losses. Most didn't see the bear market coming and thus didn't take the proper steps to prepare their portfolio for it.

I want you to step back for a moment and separate yourself from your emotional reaction to the last bear market. Imagine what you could have done differently to minimize the impact of the bear market on your portfolio.

We're going to look at ways to find opportunities in bull or bear markets, or at the very least protect ourselves and preserve our capital. Your goal should be to prepare yourself for any market conditions you may encounter. You need to create a personal plan that fits your objectives, your tolerance for risk, and your lifestyle.

TOPICS COVERED

The contents of this book address investing in bull, bear, and even sideways markets. Let's introduce you to the topics we will address.

EMOTIONS

First, we will focus on the emotions of investing. A lot of people say that the bulk of investing is not what you do in the market or with your broker, but what takes place between your ears. (And I think that sometimes it takes place in your heart, or in your gut, as well). The biggest battle most investors wage is with their emotions; and it's a lifelong battle.

TRENDS

We also want to take a look at trends. I think it is important to really understand trends. In the chapter on trends, I will give you some very specific things to help you identify trends, to be more aware of them, and to make them become a basic element of your stock research and investment decisions. This is important because it is going to help keep you out of trouble and help you stay on the right side of the market. I think you will find that this simple concept will help you choose the best strategies to employ when market conditions change. Identifying and following the correct trends can also help you protect yourself from declines in the market, which could reduce your capital and limit your ability to recover after sustaining some losses.

MANAGING YOUR RISK

We are going to remind you of one of the simplest tools for protecting yourself against sudden declines in the market—stop loss orders. Most of you have heard of them or even used them from time to time. My goal is to show you exactly how to use them and to convince you that they should always be a part of your investment strategy. One of the problems many people have after sustaining some substantial losses is that they think it is too late to do anything about it. In most cases, it is not too late. I think you need to incorporate stops into your investment program.

FINDING OPPORTUNITIES IN UP AND DOWN MARKETS

In our view, options are the best way to profit in either bull or bear markets. As we will discuss later, options can be used to enhance the profit potential of your stock holdings, or can be used as their own speculative vehicle. There are plenty of ways to profit in a bear market for those who wish to apply bearish strategies, while others are only appropriate for bull markets.

In bull markets, there are two methods we will discuss, call-option buying and covered-call writing. One is more speculative, although the risk is clearly defined. The second is a more conservative approach that allows the investor to collect income and still profit from their stock's appreciation.

There are two bear-market approaches we're going to address: using put options and shorting stock. We will take a good look at put options. This is a strategy most investors don't understand—and when people don't understand something, they tend to avoid it. Now is a great time for you to learn how to recognize opportunities for trading puts. My goal is to help you completely understand the basic skills needed to become a confident put player.

In addition to being a put player, there is another approach that you can use that does not involve options. This is referred to as "shorting stock." Although many of you have heard of the term, I am going to define it and discuss its pros and cons. However, I consider the strategy of selling short to be a lot more aggressive than that of buying puts, which means my focus will be more towards the put plays than short selling.

Most investors are not well suited for short selling because of the additional risk involved. With option plays, we are able to limit our risk and keep it to a very specific amount. We will look at put options in two different ways: first, by using them to profit from declines in the market, and second, by using them as an insurance policy to protect the stock positions you have in your account. Both are valid ways to use put options, and we want to cover both of them so that you can have the confidence to incorporate them into your individual portfolio.

COLLARS

The final thing we want to talk about in this book is a strategy that is used in sideways or down-trending markets. It is called a "collar." This is a strategy that has been around for a long time. It is one of the most simple and conservative option strategies available. A collar is basically a way of structuring an option trade so that you get free insurance against a decline in a stock you own. A collar functions as a hedge against sudden declines in a stock. It's also possible to profit from a collar depending on what the stock does after you apply the strategy, so it's a dual purpose strategy offering great protection for a very low cost and the potential for a small gain if the stock rises.

We talk about puts as having value in terms of protecting ourselves against declines in the market or declines in an individual stock, but I will show you a simple way to actually generate from your investments—all the money it takes to buy these insurance policies. Just remember, it's called a collar and I am sure you are probably asking, "Why hasn't anybody ever told me about this before now?"

CHAPTER 1

DON'T LET THE BEAR SCARE YOU

WHY BULL & BEAR MARKETS?

No one is really sure where the terms bull and bear markets came from and the majority of today's investors have never lived through a real bear market. This uncertainty makes most of us uneasy and, therefore, afraid.

In a bull market, like the one we have experienced since the early 1990s, stocks move higher, the economy is growing at a strong pace, jobs are readily available, and inflation is generally not a problem. Bull markets, by definition, are a period of rising demand for stocks and decreasing supply. Positive investor psychology obviously plays a role, as does the government's action to stimulate the economy, either through policy enactments or a stimulative Federal Reserve policy.

Bear markets, on the other hand, are periods of rising supply of stocks and diminishing demand. Investor sentiment is pessimistic as stocks are falling, and the majority expects them to continue declining. Unemployment generally is rising and economic production is falling. By the time the bear market ends, many investors are so discouraged that they swear they will never again invest in the stock market.

To qualify as a bull or bear market, the major averages need to move 20 percent or greater in the same direction. The cycle of bull and bear markets is found throughout the last 100 years and many would argue that the phenomenon can be traced back much further. One of the longest running bull markets has occurred over the past six to ten years. The start of bull markets is always a point of debate, but the frenzy of buying that terminated in early 2000 had all the requirements of a speculative bull market top. There have been other major bull markets, in the 1980s, the late 1960s to early 1970s and of course in the roaring 20s. They all ended in market crashes and/or economic recessions. They also created tremendous opportunities. Depending on the criteria used there have been between 25 and 28 bear markets in the last 100 years.

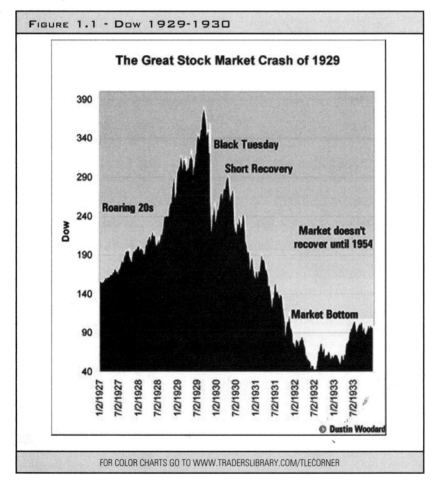

FIGURE 1.1 - DOW 1929-1930

The Great Stock Market Crash of 1929

FOR COLOR CHARTS GO TO WWW.TRADERSLIBRARY.COM/TLECORNER

The only bear market that most investors today are aware of is the one that coincided with the stock market crash of 1929 and the Great Depression (see Figure 1.1). From the 1929 highs, the Dow Jones Industrial Average, which was the primary market average, gave up about 90 percent of its value in just a three-year period. If you read the newspaper clippings from the period, some of the comments will sound eerily similar to those heard in late 1999 and early 2000. For example:

Business Week, September 27, 1929 "For five years at least, American business has been in the grip of an apocalyptic, holy-rolling exaltation over the unparalleled prosperity of the 'new era'."

As you might recall, one of the reasons the market couldn't go down in 2000 was that things were different this time and the Internet phenomenon changed everything. In fact, you will find comments similar to the one above that coincide with every bull market top in recent memory.

In recent history, the most severe bear market occurred in 1973-74, where the major averages lost up to 48 percent and some of the popular mutual funds of the time lost over 80 percent of their value.

Over the past 50 years, the average bear market has resulted in a 29 percent drop in prices and has lasted about nine months. The aforementioned 1973-74 bear market lasted 20 months while the 1968-1970 bear market dragged on for 18 months. On average, since 1950, it has taken the market averages 17 months to regain 100 percent of their value. Once again, on the extreme side, was the 1973-74 market, as it took over five years before the losses were recovered.

The educated investor must acknowledge that there are bull and bear markets and that they must learn the skills to take advantage of both types of market behavior. Equally important, one should not get too discouraged by bear markets, as bear markets, like bull markets, create tremendous profit opportunities if one has the proper skills.

REVIEW

1. A bear market is described as a decline of more than _20_ percent in the major stock market indexes.

2. Over the past 50 years, the average bear market has resulted in a _29_ percent market decline and lasted approximately _9_ months.

3. The most recent bear market began in March of _2000_.

4. Bear markets are typically followed by _Bull_ markets.

5. Over the past 50 years, the market has taken on average _17_ months to recover 100 percent of the value lost in a bear market.

FOR ANSWERS GO TO: WWW.TRADERSLIBRARY.COM/TLECORNER

CHAPTER 2

EMOTIONS OF INVESTING

L et's step back, take a deep breath, and look at the overall market. I want you to make an assessment of the emotions you felt that last time the market dipped. How did it make you feel? What did you do with your investments? Do you look back and wonder how you made some of the decisions you made? Clearly emotions have a big impact on our decision making when it comes to our money and investments. In this chapter we're going to take a look at how our emotions impact our decisions and how we can manage them to make better decisions when emotions are high.

Without question, the biggest challenge most investors face is controlling their emotions. Everyone has a point where they cross over the line of reason and logic and allow their emotions to take over. If we could somehow identify where that point is, we could become better at avoiding it.

The point where you cross over that line is not something you can figure out in your head. We know when we have crossed the line because we feel it in the pit of our stomach. I am confident that you know that feeling I'm talking about.

It's when you wake up at 3:00 a.m. and turn on the television to CNBC to check the S&P futures to see if you can get a read on whether the market will open up or down that day. It's when you're out with your family and all you can think about is how you're going to break the news to your spouse that you lost the bulk of your children's college funds.

We all know the feeling of being in a situation where there appears to be no way out—so we do the natural thing and panic. Only after making a hasty decision, do we finally realize that we usually bought or sold at the worst possible time. Emotions cloud your judgment . . . and if ever you need a clear head, it's when you're making a decision about your money.

FEAR AND GREED

It is very important that you understand there are many different emotions involved in investing. The two primary emotions are fear and greed. In a bull market it's our overwhelming sense of greed that drives most of our investment decisions. We become confident—we think everything is going up. We have become part of the crowd and are simply buying because everyone else is—and everyone seems to be making money no matter what he/she buys.

> Fear is a far more powerful emotion than greed for most investors. While greed gets us into the market when an opportunity may be minimal, fear will keep us out of a market when the opportunities are plentiful. Greed creates losses and fear creates lost opportunity.

In a bear market, fear takes over and you become controlled by that emotion. I think fear is a far more powerful emotion than greed for most investors. While greed gets us into the market when an opportunity may be minimal, fear will keep us out of a market when the opportunities are plentiful. Greed creates losses and fear creates lost opportunity. When the majority of investors are feeling these emotional extremes, it's usually a signal that the market has hit either a top or bottom, or at least it's getting close.

Fear is the emotion most often associated with bear markets. Most of us are afraid of losing money, and if you're not, you probably should be. The fear of losing money can be paralyzing. I have spoken with many people who have bought a stock and have held onto it for a long period of time. They are classic buy-and-hold investors, and they have convinced themselves that they can ride out any downturn in the market. They have confidence the market will recover from any dip.

There is nothing wrong with investing for the long haul, but, unfortunately, in a bear market many of those investments can decline 10, 20, 30, 40—or even as much as 90 percent. If you're still holding one of those e-commerce stocks that were all the rage in 1999, you know the feeling. The last bear market didn't stop with just the weak companies. Even the market leaders like Cisco, Intel, Dell, and Microsoft were trading for much, much less in 2002 than they were at the beginning of 2000.

Most investors whose portfolios were severely damaged in the last bear market never took advantage of the many warning signs that the market was changing. Greed also played a large part in this, as suddenly a 100 percent gain was not enough, nor a 200 percent . . . let's hold out for 300 percent. When it becomes too easy to make money on your investments, complacency and greed take over. Of course, if you become successful in bear market strategies, greed can also play a role. In my experience, I've noticed that the best investors tend to be almost mechanical in their approach to investing. While one can never totally eliminate emotions from investing decisions, successful investors are able to minimize their impact.

RECOGNIZING THE WARNING SIGNS

In Spencer Johnson's book, *Who Moved My Cheese?*[1], the main characters search through a maze that symbolizes life to find cheese that is symbolic for happiness, money, and success. They search hard and finally find the cheese. Each day they return to enjoy the cheese. Life is good.

Then, one day, there is no more cheese. But it wasn't a sudden event. Each day the supply of cheese dwindled. Some recognized this trend and began to search

---

[1] *Johnson, Spencer. Who Moved My Cheese? An Amazing Way to Deal with Change in Your Work and in Your Life. New York: G. P. Putnam and Sons, 1998.*

the maze for more cheese. The other characters didn't recognize these changes and found themselves in a state of shock when the cheese finally disappeared.

While the one group immediately took off into the maze and eventually found a new supply of cheese, the other group sat around wondering who moved the cheese and hoping it would magically show up again. It never did, and they, too, eventually had to enter the maze and begin to search for more cheese.

Compare the cheese to stocks—stocks people own that drop in value. They fail to see the changes that happen along the way and then feel surprised when their stocks are no longer doing well. They wonder who moved the cheese.

Had they been more aware of the changing trends in the market, they could have better prepared themselves for the drop. They could have taken precautionary measures to protect their investments from loss.

Too many investors fall in love with their stocks and lose sight of the fact that they own stocks to make money. When the opportunity to make money is gone, they need to look to a new stock for a better opportunity or simply move to the sidelines and be happy to earn some interest on their money until the opportunity returns.

GETTING OFF THE TRAIN

Changing trends are a lot like a train traveling across the country. Let's call this the "losing train." It doesn't just go from point A to point B; it makes lots of stops along the way. Each time the losing train stops, the conductor asks the passengers if they want to get off. Most choose to stay on. When the train finally gets to point B, the passengers are wondering how they could have stayed on it for so long when there were so many opportunities to depart, especially since the train was clearly not headed in the direction they intended to go.

The paralyzing nature of fear causes us to avoid making hard decisions. This delay usually ends up compounding an already bad situation. We hold onto a stock for so long that we finally decide it's too late to do anything. We continue to hold our investment, like a lottery ticket, hoping there will be some miraculous recovery. The recovery rarely comes. These trades are the ones that usually result in those catastrophic losses.

As I travel the country talking to investors, I often ask if they could have done better last year, by two or three percent on their overall portfolio, had they simply eliminated one or two bad investments. It's amazing to see an entire roomful of investors nod their heads in the affirmative. One of the easiest ways to build a portfolio is to avoid the catastrophic losses we so often seem to create. What kind of impact could earning an extra 2 to 3 percent each year by eliminating just one bad investment have on your portfolio over your investing lifetime?

It is amazing that the majority of these people say they knew they should have gotten out, but didn't. Most of them were paralyzed by fear or had a lack of confidence in their own ability to read a chart and make a decision. This kept them in the investment far longer than they had ever intended.

Let's take a look at why someone would hold onto any investment as it declined by 30, 40, 50, or 60 percent, instead of closing it out with just a 10 to 15 percent decline. Is it in hopes of the investment bouncing back? In order to analyze this, we need to look at the individual aspects of fear, and break them down.

ADMITTING YOU'RE WRONG

The first thing to look at is the fear we all have of losing money. Nobody likes to lose money. Often our emotions make us stay in an investment, even though we know that it may not be the best place to be. Sometimes we just can't come to grips with accepting that we have lost money and this keeps us in a position longer than we should be.

> **Often our emotions make us stay in something, even though we know that it may not be the best place to be.**

The next thing, which I am sure many of you have experienced over the last couple years with the market going up, is the fear of giving back a profit. Now ask yourself if you have ever been in a position where a stock went in your favor and created a profit, but then you were so afraid of giving that profit back that you sold too soon. Then, when the stock continued to run a long way beyond that, you were on the sidelines kicking yourself for getting out too quickly. Fear also kept you from getting back in, because you convinced yourself that the investment would drop the minute you did.

It was the fear of giving back the profit that caused you to make an emotional decision to get out too early. Maybe there wasn't any real reason or any signal on the indicators or graphs, or anything on the news you were following that said, "Get out now." But your simple fear of giving back your profit caused you to sell.

> **Lossess do not always mean you've made a mistake. Losses are as much a part of investing as profits. It's how you deal with them that determines your long-term success or failure.**

Giving back a paper profit feels a lot like having a stranger reach into your pocket and help themselves to a few dollars from your billfold. You feel violated or robbed. It's the fear of this situation that motivates many investors to cash out of great investments long before the full benefit of their wise decision is realized. We've all heard the saying: "Let your profits ride and cut your losses short." Unfortunately, many investors do just the opposite, they "Let their losses run and cut their profits short."

Selling too soon is better than selling too late, but I'll discuss that later. We also recognize that when we get into a trade that is working out, we want to stay in it as long as we can. This is when greed can take over your emotions, and the original target of a 20 percent gain is not enough as you shoot for 50 percent, and then 100 percent. Soon you have no profit at all. Then the next time you will likely overreact, as the fear of giving back your profits leads to an emotional decision to get out too early.

The last thing is admitting you were wrong. It is not a pleasant experience to have to admit that you've made a mistake. But you need to realize that not being honest with yourself will usually just compound the problem. You shouldn't take these things personally.

The fact is, you can do everything right, you can do everything you've been taught, and everything you have learned on your own —and you can still lose money. You can apply everything you know about investing, and you are still not guaranteed success, even if you do it perfectly right.

There are always things that surprise us—things that change the picture. It's how you adapt to the change that will determine whether change becomes a roadblock or a speed bump on the way to accomplishing your investment objectives. The sign of a really disciplined investor is one who can quickly admit a mistake, take a small loss and move on. Many investors take losses personally. They think that if they sell, their spouse or broker will find out about it, and be disappointed or make fun of them. Clearly, our pride often gets in the way of making good decisions with our money.

Losses do not always mean you've made a mistake. Losses are as much a part of investing, as are profits. It is how you deal with them that determines your long-term success or failure.

At first a loss is just a number on the statement your broker sends you each month; however, when it is no longer just on paper, you have to be able to admit that you had a loss and move on. Unfortunately, for many people this is a challenge. We all need to learn to deal with losses and overcome those negative thoughts.

I think it is important for you to understand that you do not have control over the stock market; you don't have control over an individual stock or option. You don't control the mutual funds or any of the other investment vehicles you choose to invest in. You simply need to be able to monitor their movements, using the best available resources and information, and make decisions that will, hopefully, keep you on the right side of things.

ETERNAL OPTIMISM

There is one other emotion I want to point out that is a little more subtle. It is the pitfall of being an eternal optimist. I don't think there is any doubt that most people who invest in the market do so because they want to buy something and see it go higher.

I got my first securities license in 1987. Some of you will remember that year as one of the most volatile in the history of the market. That was the year of "Bloody Monday" in the stock market, when the Dow fell over 500 points in a single day. I think you'd agree that starting out in the financial services industry in this type of environment would be a real challenge. I noticed quickly that the investment strategies producing profits when the market was falling were the ones that were working the best. I wondered why more of the brokers in the office weren't selling these investments to their clients.

One day I stopped into the sales manager's office to discuss this idea I had. I thought I could increase my production by changing from selling bullish investments to selling bearish investments. This seasoned manager put his arm around me and said he agreed with my assessment of the market and was even doing some of these things in his personal account with his own money.

He then went on to tell me that people want to buy things that will go up in value. He said it was the "American way." He also told me that the minute I stopped selling dreams, I wouldn't be able to sell a thing. It didn't make any sense to me. All the other brokers continued to encourage their clients to buy more and average down. I chose to leave the industry and just focus on my own account.

There is a powerful motivation to be invested in the market all the time, and in a bull market we get complacent. We often ignore the signals that are in front of us and continue to apply bullish strategies, even though the market is clearly bearish. We keep trying to pick the bottoms, and the bottoms keep dropping out. When you find yourself hoping, wishing, and praying for things to get better, that's a sure sign you've fallen prey to your emotions. Sometimes being in cash is a pretty good strategy. Don't believe me? Just ask any of those investors that lost 80 percent in Nasdaq stocks in the last bear market if they would have preferred the returns on a savings account at their local bank and you'll get the answer.

FIGHTING THE TREND

The eternal optimist is one who ignores changing trends and continues to apply bullish strategies in bearish markets. If you're not willing to adjust your approach when the market trends change, you need to at least recognize the change and move to the sidelines and wait it out. Those who can't overcome their bullish tendencies could lose it all before the market turns positive again. Some of you need to look back and ask yourself, "Over the last year, would I have been better off sitting with my money in cash and earning interest on it, even if it was just in a money market account making 4 to 5 percent a year?"

Would that have produced a better return than what you made in the stock market over the same period? Some of you may, unfortunately, have to say yes. So that's the challenge. And, we are not admitting defeat by moving our money out of stocks and putting it in more conservative investments like bonds or interest-bearing money market accounts. This idea is something people have to overcome. We have been spoiled with the 20 percent, or better, returns in the market over the past few years. Now we must be content with a more conservative rate of return on our money.

Any return is better than a loss, in my book. I want to focus my investments where there is the best opportunity for portfolio growth and to avoid losses. If that's in a money market account, so be it.

Let's recap the key points of managing our emotions:

THE EMOTIONS OF INVESTING

FEAR

- Of losing money
- Of giving back a profit
- Of admitting you're wrong

GREED

- Expecting unreasonable profits
- Becoming overconfident

ETERNAL OPTIMISM

- Fighting the trend

The more you are able to control your emotions and limit their impact on your investment decisions, the better investor you will become.

REVIEW

1. The most powerful emotion investors feel is _FEAR_.

2. The opposite emotion of fear is _GREED_.

3. The most common reaction to fear is doing _NOTHING_

4. One of the easiest ways to improve your overall returns each year is to eliminate the _CATASTROPHIC_ losses from your portfolio.

5. The fear of giving back a profit often results in selling _TOO SOON_.

FOR ANSWERS GO TO: WWW.TRADERSLIBRARY.COM/TLECORNER

CHAPTER 3

THE TREND IS YOUR FRIEND

A number of years ago I accompanied a group of Boy Scouts on a river-rafting trip to the beautiful Salmon River, in Idaho. Our guide was a veteran of hundreds of trips down the river in rafts, riverboats, and canoes. He knew every little twist and turn along the way.

The night before our journey down the river began, our guide talked to us at length around the campfire about the many things that could go wrong in order to help us prepare for the challenges that lay ahead. However, the Scouts were more interested in roasting their hot dogs and marshmallows than in listening to this wise guide.

He talked about the power of a river as it moves through the canyons. He mentioned dozens of times that it's impossible to fight the current. He told us that if we tipped over and found ourselves in the water, we should not try to swim against the current, but keep our feet forward and be on the lookout for oncoming objects, so as to avoid crashing into them. He said that to get out of the current, you must swim with it and work your way to safety on the banks.

We enjoyed two days of running the river without any incident. It was great fun for everyone. After going through increasingly difficult rapids without any trouble, our confidence in our ability was high. We began taking bigger and bigger risks, much to the dismay of our overly cautious guide.

All that changed when the raft I was guiding got caught in a hole in one of the largest rapids and shot straight up in the air like a rocket, sending all of us into the icy, churning waters. Just imagine slamming on the brakes of your car and how it throws you forward—that's what it was like.

Our confidence immediately turned to terror as each of us struggled to keep our heads above the water and swim towards the upside-down raft. Two of the boys and I were unable to reach the raft before being swept downstream in the swift-moving current.

I consider myself a strong swimmer, but even with the help of a life jacket it was difficult to stay above the thrashing current. One of the boys was able to reach a calm spot in the rapids and swim to the bank, but the other boy and I were still stuck in the middle of the river and were unable to get out of the current. No matter how hard I tried, I could not catch up to the young boy who was now over 100 feet ahead of me. He was terrified—and it was the most helpless feeling I had ever experienced not to be able to help him get out of the current.

> Fighting the trend is as difficult as trying to swim upstream in the Salmon River. You may be able to hold your ground for a minute or two, but eventually the trend will win and sweep you away with it.

About this time, one of the other leaders raced past us in a truck on the shore and threw a line across a narrow stretch of the river a few hundred yards in front of the young Scout, to give him something to grab onto as he swept by in the current. Seeing that the boy was going to be rescued, I made one last effort to swim to shore. Expending all the energy I could muster, I eventually was able to break the bond of the current and swim into some calm water near the bank. It wasn't until I was in water that was barely a foot deep that I was able to stand up. I had tried several times, but was instantly knocked down by the swift current.

I learned a valuable lesson from this terrifying experience: it's almost impossible to fight the current. The power of the current is deceptively strong. It was only when I swam with the current that I was able to make it to the shore. No amount of effort could keep me from being pulled along by the strong current.

In many respects, the stock market is also like the river. There is a current that flows, constantly pulling individual stocks up and down with it. It's subtle at times, and like raging rapids at others. The key to survival for investors in the market is to recognize the current, respect its power, and apply strategies that benefit from the direction of the flow.

In the market, the current is called the trend. You may not realize it, but the trend is as powerful as any current or tide. Fighting the trend is as difficult as trying to swim upstream in the Salmon River. You may be able to hold your ground for a minute or two, but eventually the trend will win and sweep you away with it.

THE TREND IS YOUR FRIEND

When I went through training as a new broker, I heard the saying, "The trend is your friend" at least a hundred times. I thought I knew what it meant, but it wasn't until I had lost tens of thousands of my own hard-earned money that I really understood what it meant to make the trend your friend.

I think this is one of the most fundamental aspects of investing in the stock market, and I want to take a few minutes to make sure you understand how to recognize trends and choose a strategy that will work in the current market conditions.

Each day before I go looking for new investments, I make a quick check of the major trends in the overall market, the leading sectors, and the stocks I'm following or invested in. It's the first thing I do every time I turn on the computer to look at my investments. Before I put any money at risk, I want to know which direction the current is moving so I can find the best stocks and apply the appropriate strategy.

I accomplish this task with a simple process using bar charts that you can easily duplicate in any charting program or at any of the hundreds of websites that offer charting applications. Just bring up a graph of the Dow and NASDAQ with a 30- or 50-day moving average. Personally, I like to use a 21-day moving average as that is the average number of trading days in a typical month and it's a little more sensitive to the short term swings in the

FIGURE 3.1 – UP-TRENDING CHART (STOCKINVESTOR.COM)

Potash Corp   Last: 159.04   +3.44   (0.00%)

03/06/2008, H:162.20, L:158.69, O:161.14, C:159.15

FOR COLOR CHARTS GO TO WWW.TRADERSLIBRARY.COM/TLECORNER

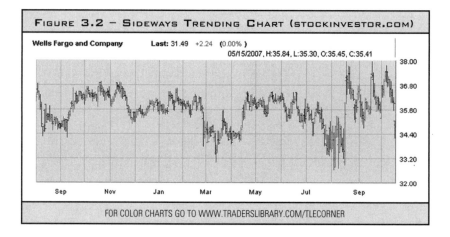

FIGURE 3.2 – SIDEWAYS TRENDING CHART (STOCKINVESTOR.COM)

Wells Fargo and Company   Last: 31.49   +2.24   (0.00%)

05/15/2007, H:35.84, L:35.30, O:35.45, C:35.41

FOR COLOR CHARTS GO TO WWW.TRADERSLIBRARY.COM/TLECORNER

FIGURE 3.3 – DOWN-TRENDING CHART (STOCKINVESTOR.COM)

Bear Stearns Companies Inc   **Last:** 10.85   +0.24   (0.00%)

03/07/2008, H:73.00, L:68.30, O:68.71, C:70.08

175.00

140.00

105.00

70.00

35.00

10.85

0.00

May   Jul   Sep   Nov   Jan   Mar

FOR COLOR CHARTS GO TO WWW.TRADERSLIBRARY.COM/TLECORNER

market. I look at the chart and determine the basic direction of the index, and of its moving average, to help me decide whether the market is moving up, down, or sideways. Don't try to be too technical here. Just visually determine the general direction the 21-day moving average is headed, going from left to right. Here are a few examples to give you the general idea (Figures 3.1, 3.2, and 3.3).

Instinctively, I'm always looking for the best time to buy stocks. That's the nature of most investors—we're always looking for stocks to buy in hopes that they will rise in value. A quick glance at the graphs I pull up, and at their moving averages, will determine if I should behave bullishly, bearishly, or stay neutral.

Once I get a feel for the overall trend in the broad market, I may use the same approach to check some of the leading market sectors—like technology, retail, banking, or oil stocks. By "drilling down" to the best sectors, I can identify the best groups of stocks to focus on, and thus isolate buying opportunities in any market. This whole process can be done in less than five minutes and can help me focus my energies on the sectors offering the best opportunities.

A simple way to evaluate the strength of the major sectors of the market is to use Exchange Traded Funds (ETFs) that are designed to follow these major sectors. I like to use the S&P Sector SPDR ETFs for this purpose. Below are a list of the symbols and the sectors they follow.

The Nine S&P Select Sector SPDR Funds Are:

- The Consumer Discretionary Select Sector SPDR Fund - XLY
- The Consumer Staples Select Sector SPDR Fund - XLP
- The Energy Select Sector SPDR Fund - XLE
- The Financial Select Sector SPDR Fund - XLF
- The Health Care Select Sector SPDR Fund - XLV
- The Industrial Select Sector SPDR Fund - XLI
- The Materials Select Sector SPDR Fund - XLB
- The Technology Select Sector SPDR Fund - XLK
- The Utilities Select Sector SPDR Fund - XLU

If I determine the trend is not favorable, it's easy to turn off the computer and head to the golf course. Both my experience in the river and my many mistakes with my own investments have taught me that fighting the trend is almost always a losing battle. I consider a day on the golf course a whole lot more fun than losing money in the market.

In my seminars, I tell my students that finding a great stock in a bear market can be a bit like finding a needle in a haystack. It's hard work. In a bull market, great stocks are plentiful and much easier to find. Just look at all the new investors who made huge profits by following the crowd and buying Internet stocks in 1999. They may not have had any idea what they were doing, but it seemed like every stock was going up, and the only way to lose was to not buy anything, as the upward current was strong.

It was hard to lose, and confidence was high—just like ours after two days of running the river. Then, in March of 2000, the raft overturned and investors found themselves swimming against the icy current, unable to swim to shore. They kept buying the same stocks hoping things would change, but this was swimming against the trend and it only compounded their losses and frustration.

For those who failed to change their approach and adapt to the new trend in the market, they most likely ended up wiping out several years of profits in just a few short months. Only those who changed their strategy to one that worked in the new market conditions could begin to take back control of their portfolio. The river and the market have many similarities. Failing to recognize changing trends can result in a financial drowning.

So how can you spot the trends in the market and adjust your approach to make sure it's following the trend? I think the easiest way is to use charts and simple moving averages to identify trends and recognize when they change.

As I mentioned earlier, I like to identify three specific trends—market, sector, and stock—before I go looking for new investments. Once you recognize the trend, it's important not to fight it, but invest with it.

SPOTTING TRENDS

I like to use moving averages to spot trends in the market, sectors, and stocks. This method is fast and easy once you know what you're looking for, and it will keep you out of a lot of trouble if you use this tool to help determine where and how you invest your money.

There are three possible trends you can see:

- Up

- Down

- Sideways

If the trend is not clear to you, the best advice is to sit out until you see it clearly. My motto is, "When in doubt, sit out."

Depending on whether you're a long or short-term investor, you may need to change the moving average you use to help you identify the trend. Short-term investors—those who don't mind moving in and out of investments every few weeks or months—may use a 30-day moving average to identify trends that help them make their decisions.

Longer-term investors, the buy-and-hold crowd, should use longer moving averages, such as a 200-day moving average. The shorter the moving average, the more sensitive it is to changes in the market. These changes could provide you with entry and exit signals on your individual investments.

Longer-term investors are not worried about moving in and out on every swing in the market, but want to stay invested as long as the major long-term trend stays intact. By using a longer-term moving average, the trend changes will be fewer and farther between. The longer-term moving average will smooth out the ups and downs in the market or stock and give fewer buy-and-sell

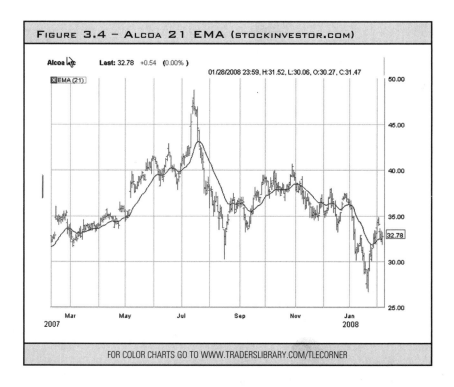

FIGURE 3.4 – ALCOA 21 EMA (STOCKINVESTOR.COM)

FOR COLOR CHARTS GO TO WWW.TRADERSLIBRARY.COM/TLECORNER

signals. So, the first thing you need to do is pick a moving average that fits your approach and objectives.

USING A 21-DAY MOVING AVERAGE TO DETERMINE SHORT-TERM TRENDS

Let's look at an example. Figure 3.4 is a one-year graph of Alcoa (AA) with a 21-day moving average plotted on it. The moving average is the smooth solid line that follows the daily movements of the stock. Notice how it smoothes out the jagged movement of the stock.

Let's follow the moving average from the left to the right of the chart and see if we can't determine the trend of Alcoa. At the far left side of the graph you can see the stock is dramatically moving up and the moving average is pointing straight upward. This is clearly an uptrend. Around the middle of July, Alcoa (AA) crosses the 21-day moving average and begins to roll over and point down. This is the start of a short downtrend that lasts for about two months before the stock once again crosses the moving average, this time moving up through it.

The stock then moves down for about a month in November and then bounces back and forth across the moving average for the month of December in a sideways trend. Notice how the moving average line flattens out while the stock is bouncing up and down in a tight range. The stock breaks down in January and violates its moving average. The stock begins another pronounced downtrend, and the moving average acts like a ceiling.

USING A 200-DAY MOVING AVERAGE TO DETERMINE LONG-TERM TRENDS

Let's look at the same stock with a longer-term moving average to see how the long-term trend differs from the short-term trend.

Using a one-year chart with a 200-day moving average, you can see that the long-term trend of Alcoa (AA) changed only once (Figure 3.5).) The trend was

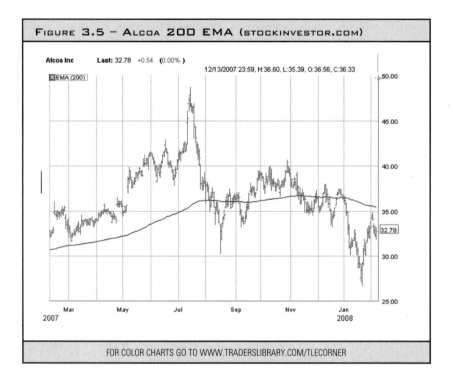

FIGURE 3.5 – ALCOA 200 EMA (STOCKINVESTOR.COM)

Alcoa Inc   Last: 32.78 +0.54 (0.00%)

12/13/2007 23:59, H:36.60, L:35.39, O:36.56, C:36.33

EMA (200)

50.00
45.00
40.00
35.00
32.78
30.00
25.00

Mar   May   Jul   Sep   Nov   Jan
2007   2008

FOR COLOR CHARTS GO TO WWW.TRADERSLIBRARY.COM/TLECORNER

up for most of the year in spite of a very volatile spike down in July and then leveled out in a sideways trend for the balance of the year..

If you use the moving average as your guide, you can easily spot the trend in an index or stock. Once you know the trend, it's easier to pick the right strategy and take advantage of it.

DON'T FIGHT THE TRENDS

Here are some strategies to employ during the different trends you might see in the market:

- When the trend is up, choose bullish strategies, like buying stock or call options.

- When the trend is sideways, hold onto your present investments and consider option-selling strategies that generate income during these trendless times in the market.

- If the market is trending down, use bearish strategies, like buying puts or shorting stock, in order to capitalize on the trend.

A note about technical indicators: I like to use technical indicators to help make timing decisions on my investments. My company's web site www.stockinvestor.com has some unique color-coded arrows (represented here as up and down arrows) that help identify the breakouts and breakdowns in a stock, as measured by a host of commonly used technical indicators. From my classes, I get the impression that many want to trust technical

FIGURE 3.6 – DELL AND NASDAQ (STOCKINVESTOR.COM)

Dell Inc   Last: 19.43   +0.36   (1.89%)

11/07/2007 23:59, H:30.06, L:29.17, O:29.97, C:29.31

NASDAQ Composite Index

NASDAQ

FOR COLOR CHARTS GO TO WWW.TRADERSLIBRARY.COM/TLECORNER

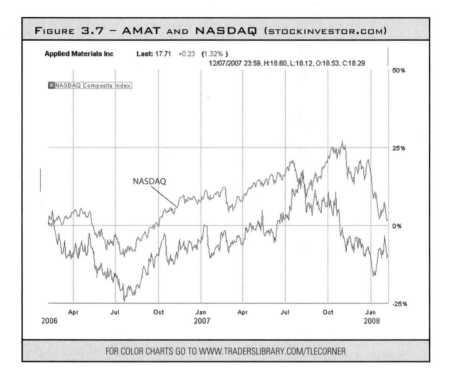

indicators more than trends. This is a dangerous thing to do. Trends should ALWAYS be given a higher priority in your decision-making process than any technical indicator.

Take a look back at the last few poor investments you've made and see if you made the mistake of ignoring the trend over another piece of information. I'll bet you'll find that the majority of stocks you lost money on were ones you bought when the trend was down. You can't expect to make money if you're trying to swim against the current. The current always wins.

Let's look at a couple of graphs which illustrate this fact. I have combined the NASDAQ Composite Index with the chart of Dell Computer, as well as Applied Materials (Figures 3.6 and 3.7, respectively). Notice how the highs and lows of these market leaders correspond to the entire NASDAQ market. Hopefully, you're starting to see what I mean when I say the trend is your friend.

In a moment I'm going to give you a simple three-step process for screening stocks using trends, but first I want to teach you an important lesson.

MOVING AVERAGES

Moving averages are probably the most simple, yet under-utilized indicator in the investing world. I consider a moving average an indispensable piece of information for any investment decision. The moving average can help us identify the trend, as well as determine areas of support and resistance. These are critical pieces of information. The only drawback of using moving averages is that they are lagging indicators, meaning that they can only reflect what has already happened rather than forecast the future movement of a stock.

Figure 3.8 is the graph of the Nasdaq Composite we looked at earlier. I want you to look at it again and notice how the index seems to bounce off the moving average. Notice which way it bounces when the stock is trending up, and

FIGURE 3.8 – NASDAQ 21 EMA (STOCKINVESTOR.COM)

FOR COLOR CHARTS GO TO WWW.TRADERSLIBRARY.COM/TLECORNER

which way it bounces when the stock is trending down. Can you see how the index bounces up when the trend is up and down when the trend is down?

The index or stock and the moving average are like magnets—they constantly want to move together. When they come together, there is either going to be a breakout or a breakdown. I like to use technical indicators to help me determine which will happen. When the stock and moving average come together and the indicators show bullish signals, I play for a bounce up. When the indicators are showing bearish signals, I expect a bounce down.

It's when you try to mix trends and signals that you get into trouble. The MACD and Stochastic indicators showed bullish signals when the stock was trending down the last week on this graph, but the rally hit the moving average and quickly fell back.

These are what are commonly called "Bull Traps." They looked like a bullish breakout, but quickly changed and trapped those who placed bullish trades in a bad situation. This is just like a correction in a bullish market, but in reverse. We know the market corrects every once in a while in a bullish market, so why would it not do the same in a bearish one?

In a bullish market, the dips represent great buying opportunities. You've probably heard the "buy the dip" approach to investing. During bull markets, it's a great approach. But if you apply the buy-the-dip approach in a bear market, you're going to find yourself on the wrong side of the market more often than not.

Let's see if I can't reduce this whole discussion into something concise that you can use. Here's what I've come up with:

When a stock approaches its moving average, it tends to bounce away from the moving average in the direction of the trend of the moving average.

This rule can help you avoid the bull traps in a down market and find confidence in the bounces during a bull market. Now that you understand this concept, let me give you three simple rules that can help you apply this concept properly. I'm going to take the bullish side of things, as that's the approach most investors tend to favor.

1. Only invest in stocks with an up-trending short-term (21 Day Exponential Moving Average) moving average.

2. Only invest when the technical indicators you follow give you a bullish signal.

3. Only invest if there is no immediate overhead resistance on the chart.

I follow these simple rules when I'm looking for investments in volatile markets. It makes me very selective and keeps me on the sidelines when the current is strong. Another good indication the breakout is real is a spike in volume above the average level for that stock. Major breakouts are always accompanied by strong volume.

I put the trend at the top of the list and then I look at the indicators. I check to make sure there is no resistance to stop a rally. If I see there is a previous high or an area of congestion just above the current price, I will either pass on the trade or wait until the stock is able to close above this level before investing in it.

Shorter-term investors may see opportunities to play the bull traps with calls or buying stock. Doing this is both risky and aggressive, but if you're going to do it, get in the play when the indicators turn positive and use the down-trending moving average or any overhead resistance as your exit target. If you use this risky short-term approach, be sure to get out quickly and not hold past these exit targets.

Volume usually increases in support of a change in the trend. When the moving average starts pointing up, look for volume to increase on the up days in the market or the individual stock. If volume is weak or dropping, be very cautious or simply avoid the trade. It's just the opposite on the downside. Look for volume to increase on the down days and dwindle on the up days. This indicates support of the trend.

Let's finish off our discussion of trends by looking at some specific stocks and applying our three-step screening process. The first stock we'll evaluate is Citigroup (C).

CASE STUDIES

CITIGROUP (C)

In the last half of 2007 the financial sector was under severe pressure as the sub-prime mortgage market collapsed, taking with it many of the big names in the financial sector, like Citigroup. Many of the large banks and brokerage firm were forced to write off billions of dollars of losses related to their trading in mortgage-backed securities.

The drop in Citigroup began in June of 2007 (Figure 3.9). Let's take a look at a 2-year chart for Citigroup and focus our attention on the last short up move

FIGURE 3.9 – CITIGROUP (STOCKINVESTOR.COM)

FOR COLOR CHARTS GO TO WWW.TRADERSLIBRARY.COM/TLECORNER

in this stock that occurred from March to May of 2007. Notice that prior to that time, the stock had been trending up nicely. A top was hit in the $56 range the last week in 2006 establishing an area of resistance in the stock. The stock pulled back to $50 where it found support and made another run at the high. Let's apply our simple three step trend evaluation process to this move and see if it would have helped us avoid the severe drop that followed.

The first rule is to check the trend and clearly at this point looking back the trend was positive, but this last little dip has flattened it out a bit. The stock would pass the first test. Second, we check the indicators and all the up arrows appeared just after the stock bounced off support in the last week of April. The stock would pass the second test. Now we check the resistance and see that the stock was just a couple dollars below the previous high set in December. That's not much room for the stock to run before it would run into some selling pressure, so it would not pass our third test and we would sit out. Good thing, the stock lost more than 10 percent in the next 30 days and continued to fall by almost 50 percent over the following several months. Notice how the moving average acted as resistance each time the stock rallied to it.

The check of resistance was the only thing that would have kept us from getting into this stock at the worst possible time. This example clearly illustrates the importance on NOT trusting indicators over trends.

MICROSOFT (MSFT)

Microsoft (MSFT) broke out of a narrow range in August 2007 and steadily moved higher until busting through resistance at $32 in October on huge volume (Figure 3.10). The rally stalled at $37 and the stock pulled back to support at the $33 range, where it staged another run at the high.

Notice the arrows during the first week in December.

The stock was trending up and the arrows confirmed the breakout, as did the volume. This stock passes the first two trend tests. The third is to check

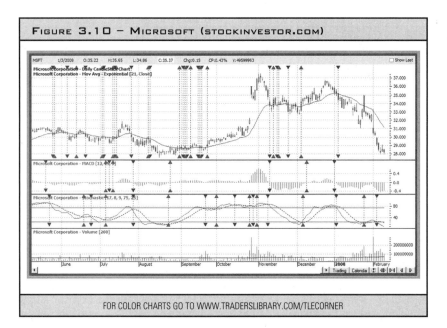

resistance. The resistance on MSFT was at the previous high of $37, and this breakout occurred with the stock trading near $34.

Knowing that there was resistance at $37, just $3 from the point of the breakout, you would have to determine if a $3 potential move was sufficient to justify playing this breakout. If you chose to play, you would certainly monitor closely when the stock approached $37 or used a price just below that as a potential profit target.

The stock ran back up just short of $37 and then pulled back a second time from this level, establishing this level as a firm level of resistance. The stock continued to decline almost 30 percent from that point.

Sometimes there is enough room to play a breakout before it hits resistance, but that area of resistance should be considered a potential exit point. If there is not enough room to generate a reasonable profit at that point, the trade should be avoided.

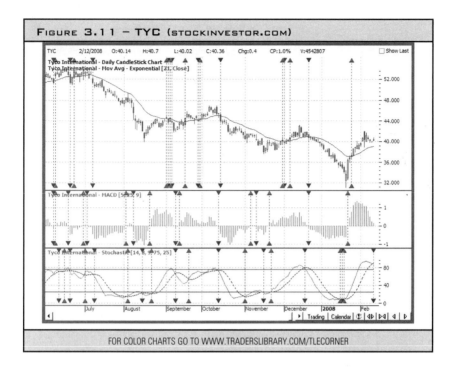

FIGURE 3.11 — TYC (STOCKINVESTOR.COM)

FOR COLOR CHARTS GO TO WWW.TRADERSLIBRARY.COM/TLECORNER

TYCO (TYC)

Tyco had a nice smooth upward trend from March through July of 2007 and then began to decline. In this example (Figure 3.11), I want to point out that during this decline the stock staged three distinct rallies in August, December, and most recently again in January 2008.

This is typical of a stock in a bearish market that makes attempts to break out and reverse the trend only to meet resistance, usually at the down-trending moving average, and fail. Each of these three rallies was accompanied by indicator breakouts, but all occurred when the stock was clearly trending down at the time. Many investors, eager to buy in a bear market, ignore the trend, and just play the breakouts as indicated by the indicators they follow. This is a dangerous approach to investing that often results in extended losses.

The key point in this example is that a down-trending moving average should be enough to keep you out of the stock no matter what the indicators are telling you. Once again, indicators are NOT more important than trends.

MARKET SECTOR ANALYSIS

To assist me in my analytical process, I created a simple portfolio of the S&P Sector SPDR ETFs.

You can easily do this on almost any financial web site that offers charting, but you'll have to look at each chart individually. By putting them all into a single portfolio, you will have quick access to them and it will only take a few minutes to complete your sector analysis.

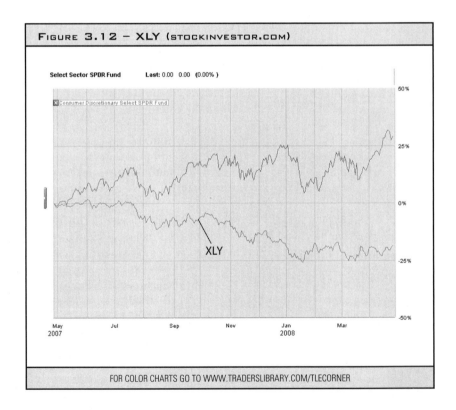

FIGURE 3.12 – XLY (STOCKINVESTOR.COM)

FOR COLOR CHARTS GO TO WWW.TRADERSLIBRARY.COM/TLECORNER

With these sector ETFs in one portfolio, you can quickly scan the bar charts of each and get a feel for the current market trends. As I mentioned earlier, this entire exercise can be done in less than five minutes each morning before the market opens. You can then focus your attention on those areas of the market that offer the best opportunities. Out of these nine major market sectors, you'll usually be able to find one or two that are moving up, no matter what the market might be doing at the time.

Figure 3.12 is a graph of the XLY (Consumer Distreationary) and the XLE (Energy) SPDR Sector ETFs These were taken at the same time and illustrate that different sectors often move in opposite directions. Notice the downtrend for the past year in the XLY and the relative uptrend in the XLE. Using these sector ETFs is a simple way to spot groups of stocks that are moving higher.

If you are looking for opportunity in Consumer Discreationary stocks, you would know today is a perfect day for a round of golf. If you are a bearish investor, you would begin your search for bearish investments. Even in the most bearish market conditions, there always seems to be one or two sectors that perform well. This is a result of money rotating from the weak sectors into the more stable ones.

SECTOR ANALYSIS

A quick look at some of the leading sector index graphs can help you identify where the money is rotating. If you're interested in playing the upside in a down market, you should at least focus your attention to the strongest performing sectors.

Here's a short list of some of the leading sectors with their index symbols. I like to instruct the students in my workshops to create a portfolio of these indexes so they can easily track the indexes' movements and spot the changes in their trends.

MAJOR SECTOR INDEXES	
Name	**Symbol**
Dow Jones Industrial Average	DJI
S&P 500	SPX
S&P 100	OEX
NASDAQ 100	NDX
Russell 2000	RUT
Internet	INX
Semiconductor	SOX
Computers	XCI
Software	CWX
Networking	NWX
Morgan Stanley Hi Tech	MSH
Banking	BIX
Broker Dealer	XBD
Healthcare	HCX
Pharmaceutical	DRG
Insurance	IUX
Oil	OIX
Retail	RLX
Airline	XAL

Become a student of the trends and you'll find that you will become a more selective investor. You'll be more patient and emotions will not have such a big impact on your decisions.

To summarize, let's review our three-step evaluation process:

THREE KEYS TO SUCCESS

1. When the trend is up, choose bullish strategies, like buying stock or call options.

   • Only invest in up-trending stocks in up-trending sectors.

   • Only invest when technical indicators you follow give you a bullish signal.

   • Only invest if there is NO immediate overhead resistance— like a moving average or a previous high or area of congestion.

2. When the trend is sideways, hold onto your present investments and consider option-selling strategies that generate income during these non-trending periods.

3. If the market is trending down, use bearish strategies, like buying puts or shorting stock in order to capitalize on the trend.

   • Only invest in down-trending stocks in weak sectors.

   • Wait until the technical indicators give you bearish signals.

   • Establish positions on rallies back to resistance, not when support or a prior low is being tested.

In a bull market, just avoiding down-trending stocks altogether should cause a dramatic improvement in your results. Don't become a bottom fisher trying to buy depressed stocks in hopes of a recovery. These stocks are weak for a reason and have a good chance of getting even weaker. Find strong stocks in uptrends. In some respects, you might need to throw out one of the oldest sayings in the market: "buy low and sell high." A better approach would be to "buy high and sell higher."

Use technical indicators on up-trending stocks to time your entry and exit. Longer-term investors should use longer-term indicators. Recognize that nearly every popular indicator is a lagging indictor and will rarely get you in at the very start of a new trend. These indicators also won't help you get out at the very top, but they generally do a good job of getting you a nice chunk out of the middle of each trend. Be satisfied with that, and you'll steer clear of many pitfalls that can reduce your returns.

Finally, be aware of resistance. That's the ceiling area where stocks tend to turn lower. The more often a stock hits a certain price and falls back, the stronger the area of resistance becomes. It will usually take a rally on higher volume to finally get through these areas and establish a new trend.

If you see overhead resistance on an otherwise strong looking stock, just be patient and wait for the stock to break through the resistance and close at a higher price. All you're usually doing when you wait like this is missing out on the first few dollars of potential. If you're shooting for the chunk in the middle, you're not too late.

REVIEW

1. The trend is your _FRIEND._

2. The trend in the market is like the _CURRENT_ in the river.

3. One of the biggest mistakes most investors make is fighting the _TREND._

4. A simple tool to help identify the trend of the market or a stock is a _BAR CHART_

5. List my three simple rules for buying a stock in a volatile market.

FOR ANSWERS GO TO: WWW.TRADERSLIBRARY.COM/TLECORNER

CHAPTER 4

RISK MANAGEMENT

Whenever I teach a workshop or speak in front of a large group of investors, I always ask them, "How many of you, looking back at the investments you made in the last year, could have done one, two, maybe three percent better on your whole portfolio by eliminating one or two really bad investments?" I don't ask them to hold up their hands because it can be kind of embarrassing for some. But I do look out and see almost all of their heads nodding in agreement—much like some of you reading this book are doing right now.

Investing is kind of like the game of golf to me. I consider myself to be a pretty decent golfer, although this is not always apparent from my score. I can play a pretty good round of golf and then have one disastrous hole. That one disastrous hole can impact my whole game, resulting in a score that doesn't reflect the fact that I just played 17 good holes.

If I can help each of you eliminate from your portfolio just one really bad trade you seem to make each year, you will do better. And that might help you to do another one, two, or three percent better each and every year. Can you imagine the difference of having that extra one or two percent, and having it compound over a lifetime of investing? What difference might that extra money make when you reach retirement age? If you could just eliminate your worst investment each year, you could easily pay for all the investor education and tools that you would ever need over your lifetime. It's the little things that often have a huge impact down the road.

If you asked any investor who has taken a catastrophic loss on an investment if they had ever intended to take that large of a loss, they would almost certainly say, "Never." You see, it's an easy decision to make when you first get into a new investment. But it's a whole different story when the investment has already dropped 10 or 20 percent.

STOP LOSS ORDERS

The time to decide to use a stop loss order is not when the market has begun to fall, but when you're considering entering a new position. Stops are one of the easiest ways to preserve your capital while keeping you out of situations in which emotions can take over and make any decision very difficult.

> **A stop loss order is an order you give your stockbroker to sell your investment if it hits a certain price that you have set as your "get-out point."**

When the markets turn and the situations change, we need to come back to the basics—"stops" being one of them. I like them because they help protect us from sudden declines in the market that we're probably not anticipating. How much could that one simple change save you over a lifetime of investing?

A stop loss order is an order you give your stockbroker to sell your investment if it hits a certain price that you have set as your "get-out point." The order is typically given to the broker at the time the initial purchase is made, or right after. It is at this point that emotions are least likely to cloud your judgment.

A stop loss order can be placed as a "Good 'Til Cancelled" (GTC) order, so that it stays in place until it either triggers and fills, or is cancelled by you or your broker. Most firms will keep a GTC order in their system for about 60 days before it automatically cancels. You will need to check the policies at your brokerage firm to make sure you know exactly how they treat GTC stop orders.

So the question is: Why don't we use these things? Why don't we put up these safety nets to help protect our portfolios against the unexpected and dramatic declines in the market place? Now I'm sure you will agree that there has been a lot of this lately—declines in the market, and those of you who understand what a stop loss is, and have used them, are probably feeling a lot better about the stock market than those who haven't used them. If you use stop loss orders, you'll be prepared when the next bear strikes.

These wise investors have preserved most of the profits they made over the last year and are now waiting to get back into the market when the opportunity presents itself again.

Let's talk about stop losses and try to get to the bottom of why people don't use them. Then, hopefully, you'll get to the point where you can make a personal commitment to incorporate them into your investing approach. It is important that you learn how and when to use them so that they work for your benefit and not to your detriment.

DETERMINE YOUR STOP FIRST

The first thing I want to point out is that we should always have a stop loss. A stop loss is what allows us to go into a trade saying, "I am willing to risk this much money if I'm wrong." This is a decision you need to make before you first get into the trade. In other words, once you get out on the high wire, when you have your money at risk in the market, you want to have a safety net already in place.

The time to decide how much we want to risk is when we are optimistic—when we think things are going to work out to our benefit. Let's face it; you're not going to get into a new investment unless you see some opportunity. The time is not after you get in and the thing starts moving, maybe even in the opposite direction that you expected. The time to set a stop loss is when you have made the decision to get into a stock. This will take away the worries such as: "What if I'm wrong? What if I'm making a mistake right now getting into this investment? How much am I prepared to lose?"

There are four ways to determine where to place your stop loss orders.

- **BY PRICE**—Setting a specific price at which you will exit the position.

- **BY PERCENTAGE**—Using a percentage, like 10 percent, to determine where you will place your stop loss order.

- **BY INDICATORS**—One example of this approach would be to choose to exit a position when the stock crosses the 21 day moving average.

- **BY SUPPORT AND RESISTANCE**—You should know where the support and resistance areas are on every stock you play and you may choose to use these areas, or breaks through these areas, as an exit point for your trade.

I am going to give you some guidelines right now, but there is nothing carved in stone on this subject. You have to individually decide what you are willing to risk. Some of you are going to be more aggressive and, therefore, will risk a larger portion of what you invest. Others will be very conservative and may wish to go to the conservative side of these ranges.

You may notice that I won't be giving you just one number. That is not the purpose of this discussion. I want you to develop your own strategy and avoid using the same strategy that I or someone else is using. You need to decide what's best for you. Investing is a very personal thing and everyone needs to have an approach that fits their personality and their individual lifestyle.

STOPS FOR STOCKS

For stocks, I want to give you the range of 10 to 20 percent of the initial purchase price. One of the great books on basic investing principles—one that I think would make a nice addition to anyone's investment library—is the book *How to Make Money in Stocks*, by William O'Neil. He is the founder of *Investors Business Daily* (IBD) newspaper. This book is a valuable resource for new investors to learn a proven approach to investing in stocks. The entire IBD newspaper is built around a simple approach called the CANSLIM method for selecting stocks.

One of the things Mr. O'Neil points out in his book is that we should all use stop losses. In his book, he recommends a 7 to 8 percent range for a stop loss on a stock. Now that is what I would consider a very tight stop, but if you are not willing to accept a lot of risk, it works well. So that is one approach.

Personally, I prefer a range of 10 to 20 percent. I would say that, for the most part, if you buy a stock and it drops 20 percent before you are able to realize any kind of a profit, you have probably made a mistake in buying that stock at the time you did. And when this happens, you need to come to grips with reality and take action to preserve your capital.

> **You have to individually decide what you are willing to risk. Investing is a very personal thing— you need to have an approach that fits your personality and your individual lifestyle.**

In a choppy market, you will be able to stay with a position longer by using a 15-20 percent stop, while the tighter 7- 8 percent stop will result in a greater number of trades and likely more frustration.

It's hard for most investors to understand that they have a better chance of earning back a loss on their next trade, than sticking with the current one in hopes that it turns around. The mistake we make is that once we have a stock go bad, we want to make sure we earn back the loss on that stock, which is not always the best decision. A better way is to preserve your capital; use the tools and resources you have at your disposal to find another investment that gives you the opportunity to make money and offset that loss. That may not be in the same stock you're currently in. It may be in a totally different investment.

Many an investor has met his/her demise waiting for that sure winner to turn around. More often than not, you will keep waiting for that stock to come back, and it never will. When you finally accept this, you're looking at one of those catastrophic losses—30, 40, or 50 percent—that will bring down the total return of your entire portfolio.

The natural tendency for someone who has suffered that kind of catastrophic loss is to go back in and say, "Now I need to apply a more aggressive strategy," or, "Now I need to buy call options to make it back that much faster." Doing this usually just compounds the problem, resulting in an even greater loss than you had in the first place.

OPTION STOPS

> In option stops, think of a stop as not having to pay to put up the safety net, but having to pay if you ever land in it.

If you're an options investor, I would suggest a stop loss range of 30 to 50 percent of the premium paid for the option. Thirty percent is actually very close for an option trade. Since a small movement in a stock can create a much larger percentage move in an option premium, you need to allow more room with options than with stocks. Keep in mind that you have already limited your total risk to the premium you pay, which is usually a small fraction of the price of a share of stock. This being the case, you have to be willing to risk a larger portion of this premium in order to avoid getting stopped out too early.

Another challenge for the option investor is that most brokers are not willing to accept any kind of stop loss order on an option, and those that do—at least most I've come across—will only accept it as a day order. Your only option in this case may be to use a mental stop. (We'll discuss this later). Only at firms that specifically cater to options investors will you usually find a policy that allows GTC stop orders on options. Some live brokers will offer this service to good clients, but generally you will give them your stop price and then trust that they will be following your position close enough to enter the order to get you out when your trigger price is reached. Those who operate like this will almost certainly warn you in advance that you're not guaranteed your stop price. It's kind of their way of saying, "I may not be watching that close." Not much comfort if you've got your hard-earned money on the line.

A day order will only last for one trading day and then it automatically expires. In order to replace your stop order, you have to re-enter it the next morning or you won't have the comfort of knowing your safety net is in place.

It doesn't cost anything to place or change a stop order. One of the biggest myths in investing is that brokers get paid a commission to "take" an order. In reality, brokers only get paid a commission to "fill" an order. A stop order only costs you money if it is executed, and this is an order we place in hopes of it never getting filled. If you place a stop and it gets filled, you are most likely going to be happy to be out of that losing investment with part of your capital. Your commission is a small price to pay for that kind of protection. Think of a stop loss order as not having to pay to put up the safety net, but having to pay if you ever land in it. I think you get the point.

Some people who trade where only day stop orders are allowed get tired of the hassle of changing or re-entering those stop orders each and every day. In other words, they get lazy and they stop using them. Most option investors end up keeping their stops in their heads as a mental stop. Let's define this term right now.

MENTAL STOPS

A mental stop is something we keep in our head. We decide where we want to cut our losses, and then we monitor our position and physically enter the sell order ourselves when that price is reached. There is nothing automated about it, and it requires constant monitoring.

For those who choose to use mental stops, I've found it very helpful to write down your desired trigger point in some type of trading journal or trade record. It just seems that writing it down makes it more real and easier to react to when the stop price is reached. That's the real weakness of a mental stop. You have to be disciplined enough to physically place the order to sell when your emotions are probably at their peak. If you find that after trying a mental stop you simply don't have the discipline to pull the trigger and get out, you should probably avoid those fast-moving or volatile investments that often result in having to make this type of decision.

A trading journal or trading record is a good idea for most investors. It is a great way to keep track of your trades and focus on the decisions you made. It's also good to record the current market conditions at the time you make each trade. You can write down the closing figures for the major indexes and any major news events of the day.

A journal is also helpful for analyzing mistakes you might have made and discovering if perhaps you had a flaw in your decision-making process. Most of us can hardly remember executing a trade—let alone what motivated us to do it. If you decide to use a trading journal, write down what you have set as your stop price each time you enter a new position. It is often said that a goal not written is only a wish. The same can probably be said of stop loss orders. You need to have them written down or placed with your broker, or they are no more than just a wish. Usually, if you write your stop price down, you will become more disciplined, and it will keep you constantly reminded of what it is.

CHOOSING YOUR STOP

The next things we are going to look at are other ways to determine where to put a stop. Most people who don't use stops will tell you that they hate getting stopped out of an investment, only to see it almost instantly rise again above their stop price. We call this getting "whipsawed," and it's something that you will eventually have to deal with if you use stops. So let's look at another way to determine where to place our stops to allow the best opportunity to stay in an investment even if it dips.

We talked a lot in Chapter Three about support and resistance. Support is an area where buyers of a stock tend to jump in and offset the selling pressure to stabilize the stock. This is a great area to place a stop. When a stock finally breaks through these areas of support, dramatic price declines often occur. Setting your stop at this level, or slightly below it, will help you get out before everyone starts rushing for the exit.

Another great way to determine where to place a stop is to follow the trend of a stock and get out when the trend is broken. If you're going to use trends as a signal to exit a position, you first need to decide how you're going to measure and track them. We discussed this in more detail in the last chapter, but let me remind you that one of the simplest ways to track a trend is by looking at the simple moving average.

> Another way to determine where to place a stop is to follow the trend of a stock and get out when the trend is broken. To track the trend, use a moving average that matches the time frame of your investment objective. For example, a 30-day works well for short-term investing, while a 200-day for long-term.

Remember to use a moving average that matches the time frame of your investment objective. A person trading the short-term moves would most likely want to follow a 21- or 50-day moving average; whereas a person wishing to invest for the long haul and ride out the small dips would most likely use a longer-term moving average, like a 200-day. The moving average should be matched to your objectives. I personally like to use a 21-day Exponential Moving Average for short-term and option plays.

If you are watching a stock and see that the stock has moved through its moving average, this would be a great time to move to the sidelines. Many investors who use mental stops like to set their stops at the moving average

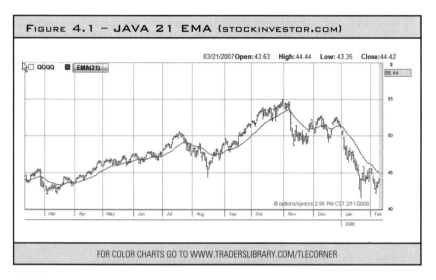

FIGURE 4.1 - JAVA 21 EMA (STOCKINVESTOR.COM)

03/21/2007 Open: 43.63   High: 44.44   Low: 43.35   Close: 44.42

FOR COLOR CHARTS GO TO WWW.TRADERSLIBRARY.COM/TLECORNER

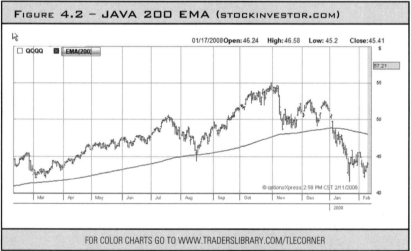

FIGURE 4.2 - JAVA 200 EMA (STOCKINVESTOR.COM)

01/17/2008 Open: 46.24   High: 46.58   Low: 45.2   Close: 45.41

FOR COLOR CHARTS GO TO WWW.TRADERSLIBRARY.COM/TLECORNER

they choose to follow. They know that if the stock breaks through their moving average, they need to place the order to get out.

Those of you who like to hold an investment for a long period of time and ride out the dips will need to use a longer-term moving average to avoid stopping yourself out before the stock is finished running. Every investor should be aware of the long-term trend of their investments, and should be able to recognize when these trends change.

The easiest way to see this—for those of you who are in more of that long-term perspective with your investments—is to look at a long-term chart. By long term, I mean more than one year. Use a three-year, five-year, or ten-year chart and apply a 200-day moving average to it. This will give you a nice long-term trend to follow. Notice that many of the stocks you look at will be way above the moving average for long periods of time. This will help you to avoid panicking at each little dip that happens along the way. But when it finally does break the 200-day moving average, (which is commonly looked at as a long-term level of support for a stock), that might be the time to say, "That's enough," and to move to the sidelines while you look for another investment opportunity.

Look at the following two graphs. Figure 4.1 is a one-year graph of Sun Microsystems with a 21-day moving average and Figure 4.2 is a one-year graph with a 200-day moving average.

The shorter-term investor, using the one-year graph and the 21-day moving average, would have moved in and out of the stock several times over the year shown. The longer-term investor, using the 200-day moving average, would have stayed in the stock until the first week in Jan 08 when the stock finally crossed the moving average.

STOP ORDER VS. STOP LIMIT

Many investors are confused when it comes to the difference between a stop order and a stop limit order. Many of the online brokers actually have two buttons you can click on their order screens that say "STOP" or "STOP LIMIT." When most investors look at this screen, the word "stop" jumps out at them. They do not pause to think what the difference is between the two.

In fact, some people reason that since they are going to put a price where they want the safety net to be, that is their stop limit, and they click the box that says "stop limit" and enter the price where they want to get out.

Now let me clarify this issue, because it is very important. A stop loss order and a stop limit order are two very different things. And it is very important that you understand the difference so you don't use the wrong one.

I am going to make a blanket statement and then explain it. Here is the simple rule: DO NOT USE A STOP LIMIT, just don't do it. What you want to use is a stop order or a stop loss order. (A safety net order.)

So what's the difference? In this case, one single word can totally change the meaning of what you're doing. Let's look at the difference.

Let's say we buy a stock for $20 and that we are willing to risk 20 percent of that. This means that the stock could drop down to $16 before we would get out. So this is where we place our stop loss order to get us out. If our broker will allow us, we would place our order good-'til-cancelled (GTC) to keep it in place without having to re-enter it on a daily basis.

The thing that would trigger our stop order is a drop in the price of the stock to $16 or less. When the $16 price is reached, at anytime the market is open, our order is triggered. The brokerage firm then sends a market order to the exchange that is filled at the current market price.

FIGURE 4.3 – MSFT GAP GRAPH (STOCKINVESTOR.COM)

FOR COLOR CHARTS GO TO WWW.TRADERSLIBRARY.COM/TLECORNER

That doesn't necessarily mean you are going to get out at $16; it just means that when the stock hits $16, the brokerage house will send a market order in to get you out at whatever the market price is when your order arrives. This may be a little above or a little below $16, but it is the $16 price that triggered the market order being sent.

Now, how is this different than the stop limit order? First, it's important that you understand what a limit order is. This can be an order to buy or sell an investment where we set the minimum price we're willing to accept. This price is our limit. A limit order is not filled unless you are able to get your limit price or a better price. So let's apply this to a stop order, as we understand it thus far.

Let's use the same example of the $20 stock with a stop at $16. Remember, our intent is to get out if the price drops to $16 or lower. If we set a stop limit at $16, and the stock goes down and hits $16, instead of a market order being sent to the exchange to sell our stock, a limit order to sell our stock at $16 or better is sent. The order to sell won't be filled unless you are able to get $16 or better, which, in this case, would be a higher price. If the market for the investment doesn't trade at, or above, your limit price, the order is not filled. So why is this important?

Let's assume the stock we own has traded down to $16.50 from the $20 price where we bought. Then, overnight, while the market is closed, the company announces a shortfall in their earnings. The next morning the stock opens up at $14. This is what is called a "gap down." The opening price is lower than the previous day's close, leaving a gap in the price chart.

Notice the gap lower in price that occurred the first week in January in MSFT stock (Figure 4.3). You can see the "gap" in the price chart from one day to the next. This is a gap down. For reference, there is also a gap up in the chart the last week in October where the price gapped higher from one day to the next.

In this case, our stop limit order would be triggered once the stock traded below $16, and our limit order to sell would be sent to the exchange. But since the stock is no longer trading at, or above, $16, it would not be filled. If the stock continues to drop, we would continue to lose more money.

Can you see how you are stuck? You have an order in—you put up the safety net—but by selecting a stop limit order rather than a traditional stop order, you specified that you are only willing to accept a sell price of $16 or better.

> **If you are going to use a stop as a safety net to sell out of an investment at a certain price, you should always use a traditional stop order and not a stop limit order.**

With a stop loss order you would be filled at the opening price and, therefore, sidestep any further price declines.

If you are going to use a stop as a safety net to sell out of an investment at a certain price, you should always use a traditional stop order and not a stop limit order. Think of them as a stop market and stop limit and it will help you to understand what the difference is. This will make your order go in as a market order and not a limit order.

A stop limit order is typically used as a buying order, not a selling order. An investor may want to buy into a stock after it reaches a certain price they've determined to constitute a new breakout, but they don't want to buy if it doesn't reach that price. They use a buy stop limit order to trigger their order at a certain price, which assures them of that price or better. This is not an order to be used by the novice investor. Experienced investors, who clearly understand what they are trying to accomplish and recognize the stop limit order as the vehicle to help them, are typically the only ones who use this type of order.

So let's review the simple rules relating to stops:

- Always set a stop when you enter a new position.

- Use traditional stop loss orders and not stop limit orders.

- Place hard stops with your broker as good til cancelled (GTC), if possible.

- If your broker does not allow GTC stop orders, use either day orders or mental stops.

- If you use mental stops, write down the stop price to help you become more disciplined.

- Set your stops on stocks somewhere in the neighborhood of 10 to 20 percent of the purchase price.

- Set your stops on option positions at 30 to 50 percent of the premium paid.

- Never lower a stop loss trigger price from your original stop price.

CONCLUSION

Everyone always talks about the value of a good education. Maybe this example will help you understand what that really means. What if you had known everything we've covered in this chapter on stops, and had applied it to the stock that you had your last catastrophic loss on? Would you still be in that stock? How much would you have saved? Hopefully, now you understand why stops are important and how easy, yet critical, they are to use.

Stop losses are very important . . . I hope you can now see that. The fact is, money saved by using a stop is just like money earned. All your past catastrophic losses are the price you've paid to learn this hard lesson. Now you'll better understand the cost of education. Nobody would ever get into an investment and plan on taking a 40 to 50 percent loss. So if you ever find yourself in that position, after reading this book, you'll have nobody to blame but the person you see in the mirror each morning.

If you find yourself in that position with one of your current investments, you need to ask yourself this simple question, "If I had the money that this investment is worth, today, in cash, would I put it into this same investment?" If the answer is no, then you know what you need to do. Sell, and move on.

— — —

REVIEW

1. The easiest way to "put up a safety net" on every investment you make is to use a _STOP_ Order.

2. A GTC order stands for _Good Til' Cancelled_

3. **TRUE OR FALSE.** You will have to pay a commission to place a stop order with your broker.

4. When is the best time to determine your exit point on a new trade. _Prior to Purchase_

5. A stop order that you keep in your head is called a _Mental Stop_

FOR ANSWERS GO TO: WWW.TRADERSLIBRARY.COM/TLECORNER

CHAPTER 5

UNDERSTANDING OPTIONS

I have a real passion for investing with options and I'm convinced that once you understand how these amazing investment vehicles work, you will too. Very few investors understand how to use options and most brokers are reluctant to recommend them because they too don't understand them and don't want to take the risk of having a customer lose money trading them.

The fact is that options were originally created to be used in very conservative ways, like hedging a position in a stock against a potential drop in value. Other investors wishing to speculate on the potential movement of a stock, use options to increase their potential profit when they are right and limit their potential loss when they are wrong.

All that being said, options can be used in both conservative and aggressive strategies, and it's ultimately up to each individual investor to determine how they fit into their individual investment plan. Most of what I do with my own money involves options. For that reason I'd like to introduce you to the basics of options in this chapter so that you can see how they can be used to both protect you and help you profit when the market turns bearish.

What is an option? An option is a contract that gives the owner the right to buy or sell a stock at a set price for a specific period of time. The key elements are that the price is fixed, and there is a specific time frame for the contract.

There are two basic types of options:

- Calls

- Puts

These two options are exact opposites:

- A Call option is the right to BUY stock at a set price, for a set period of time.

- A Put option is the right to SELL stock at a set price, for a set period of time.

To help you better understand these two basic types of options, we will compare it to real estate and then relate it back to an example from the stock market.

THE CALL OPTION

- The house is worth $100,000.

- A deal is signed (Option Contract) with the owner of the house to buy the house for $100,000 (Strike Price).

- We have the right to close the deal anytime within the next two years (Date of Expiration).

- We pay the owner $5,000, right now, to motivate him to do the deal. It is his to keep whether we buy the house or not (Premium).

- The house doubles in value over the next year. Our contract has increased in value and we can either sell the contract or exercise it to buy the home (Sell or Exercise the Option).

For a moment, let's pretend that a friend is interested in buying a home for sale, but he has neither a lot of cash, nor much credit. Without credit, getting a loan for the entire amount of property will be very difficult. And at this time, a cash sale for the entire amount of the home is impossible.

So your friend becomes a little creative. He approaches the property owner with the idea that he would like to lease the property for a period of time, and, at a future date, purchase it. In other words, the owner would retain the rights to the property and lease it to your friend for a specified time, or until it is purchased. In real estate, we refer to this kind of contract as a "lease with the option to buy."

In this particular instance, the owner has listed the property to sell for $100,000. As he reflects upon the proposal of your friend, it occurs to him that this proposal could be more profitable than an outright sale. As they sit down to write up the contract, the owner lists the sale price of the home on the contract as $100,000. At anytime during the contract period, your friend can purchase the home for that price. The two of them then decide that a period of two years will be enough for your friend to come up with the funds necessary to make the purchase.

In addition to the set price and a specific expiration date on the contract, the seller also asks for a little money to be paid up front with the contract. He explains that it is not a down payment on the property, but is a good-faith premium that will be paid now to lock in the sale price, so that only your friend can purchase the property during that two-year period. The seller asks for $5,000, which is a non-refundable premium to carry the contract.

> **The five key elements included in this real estate transaction are:**
>
> • **Option Contract**
>
> • **Strike Price**
>
> • **Date of Expiration**
>
> • **Premium**
>
> • **Sell or Exercise the Option**

Your friend calculates that since the $5,000 he will pay is non-refundable, and not a down payment on the property, he will, in essence, eventually buy the property for a total of $105,000. But today, all he has to come up with is $5,000, and he can afford to do that. Since the $5,000 gives your friend exclusive rights to that property for the next two years, he decides it is worth it.

Before signing the contract, your friend requests that one additional clause be included in the contract. This states that at any time before its expiration, your friend is allowed to sell the contract to someone else, should he decide that, for some reason, he doesn't want to buy the property, or can't purchase it. He figures by selling the contract, he might be able to get back some of the $5,000 he paid to purchase the contract, and, with any luck, perhaps even make some money on the contract itself!

Now let's see what happens over the next couple of years.

When your friend signs the contract for the property, interest rates are rather high, making it difficult for homes to sell. But after the first year of his contract, interest rates begin to fall, and, consequently, the housing market begins to take off again. He notices homes, in the area comparable to his begin selling in the $200,000 range. He begins to wonder if he can make a profit by selling the contract now that things look more favorable. Remember, your friend can buy the home for $100,000, using his contract, and then immediately turn around and sell the home for $200,000 in the current market. His profit would be $100,000 after paying off the seller. But, since he also paid a premium, he must also subtract the $5,000 he paid for the contract. Thus, his net would actually be $95,000. Not bad, considering he only put $5,000 into the deal.

Now, there is another way he can make this same kind of money without actually purchasing the property. Remember, one of the contract stipulations is that he can sell the contract to anyone else before expiration. So, if someone is interested in buying the property, he can sell his contract, giving them the right to buy the home for $100,000, while the property itself is now worth $200,000. This is a great deal, but your friend is pretty smart and realizes that if he is giving them $100,000 in equity on the property, he ought to get more than the $5,000 he paid for the contract.

In fact, the real worth of his option contract is now the difference between the price stated on the contract ($100,000), and the current price of the property (now valued at $200,000). In other words, the contract he paid $5,000 for is

now worth $100,000. So, to save time and a lot of hassle actually purchasing the property and then turning around and selling it for a profit, your friend just sells the contract to another party for $100,000 and still ends up making $100,000 minus the $5,000 initial cost of the contract, or a net profit of $95,000!

This is exactly how you can invest in the stock market. Let's look at the example below and compare the similarities to the previous example of a real estate transaction.

CALL OPTIONS ON STOCKS:

- Apple Computer (AAPL) is currently trading for $100 per share.

- We think it's going to rise in value over the next few months.

- We buy an option contract that gives us the right to purchase 100 shares of AAPL for $100 per share.

- We pay a premium of $5 per share, up front, or $500 for the contract.

- The option expires in 3 months.

- On expiration day, AAPL is trading at $140 per share.

- Our contract is now worth $40 per share, or $4,000 ($140 less $100).

- We can sell our contract or exercise it for 100 shares of AAPL.

- Our profit, either way, is $4,000, less the $500 premium we paid for the contract or $3,500.

Let us suppose we have a bullish forecast on Apple stock (AAPL) and feel that it has great potential to increase in value over the next few months. Let us also assume, for the sake of simplicity, that the Apple stock is currently trading at $100 per share.

If we purchase 100 shares of AAPL, it will cost us $10,000. That is one way to participate in the rise of AAPL stock we have forecasted. Another way is to purchase a call option contract on AAPL for a small premium over the actual purchase price of the stock. This is just like your friend who leased the house with the option to buy.

We agree to the purchase price of AAPL at $100, and set the term at three months, as it is sufficient time for our forecast to materialize. Then, we pay the premium of $5 per share for the contract. The options market is where we will locate someone to take the other side of this transaction and sell us an option. We won't get into the specifics of how this all works at this point, but rest assured that we will have no problem getting someone to take the other side in this example.

Once we pay the premium for the contract, we have the right, but not the obligation, to buy the AAPL shares for $100 anytime before the three months expires.

Let's assume that on expiration day, AAPL is now trading for $140 per share. Our forecast has become reality. Let's look at what choices we now have in order to capitalize on this situation.

> **Example 1:** As our contract stipulated, we can now "exercise" our option, or in other words, turn it into stock. We buy the shares for $100, immediately turn around and sell them in the market at the current price of $140 per share and realize a profit of $40 per share. The $5 per share we paid for this contract is deducted from our profit, so we have a net profit of $35 per share.

> **Example 2:** The other way to realize a profit is to simply find a buyer for our contract. The nice thing about the options market is that we don't have to go looking for a buyer. That's the job of the market makers. We simply say we want to sell our contract (we enter the order to sell it with a broker), and they either find some-

one to buy it or buy it themselves to make sure the market stays fair and liquid.

The price of the contract rises as the value of the underlying stock increases. Remember, we paid $5 per share for the contract up front, and now the stock is $40 per share higher than the price we "struck" our deal at, which was $100. So this option contract now has $40 per share of "equity" or Intrinsic Value as it's called in option jargon. That's the minimum it would be worth in the market. So we simply sell our contract for $40 per share in the market to get the same profit we would have earned if we exercised it, then turned it into stock and sold it at the current market price. (You will still have to deduct the cost of the contract from your profit to determine your "net profit."). This is an easier and faster way to realize a profit on an option contract and the way the majority of option investors choose to exit their trades.

The real magic in the second approach to taking your profit is in the percentage return. If you have to put up the entire $100 per share to get your net profit of $35 by exercising your option, your return will be a mere 35 percent. When you sell your contract for the same $35 net profit and all you had to put up was $5, your percentage return is substantially higher. That's the power of leverage at work.

Now, let's go over some of the language we used on the contract in both the house and stock examples. When your friend and the seller of the home signed the purchase agreement on the home, that's referred to as the strike price—the cost at which they struck the deal.

The period of time or "expiration date" in which your friend had to exercise the Lease Purchase of the home was contained in the contract. The amount he paid up front was not a down payment on the property but a "premium" paid to the seller. The premium is an amount above the actual purchase price "strike price" on the contract and is considered non-refundable. Suppose your friend had chosen to actually purchase the property rather than sell the contract, he would have "exercised the contract." Exercise signifies the physical action of purchasing the asset.

If your friend had exercised his contract, he would have done what we refer to, in the option world, as "calling" the asset away or taking possession of it. That's why with this type of option, we hope the asset appreciates so that we can purchase or "exercise our rights in the contract" at a better price than the current market price. We refer to this as a "Call Option." We hope to "CALL" it away at a more advantageous price.

As you can see, with the Call option, the purchaser has three choices:

- Choose to exercise (purchase) the asset.

- Sell the contract and let someone else purchase the asset.

- Let the option expire and just walk away without purchasing anything.

> **The key element of a call option is that it allows an investor with a bullish forecast to lock in a purchase price for a period of time by risking a fraction of the cost of the underlying shares.**

In the last instance, this may happen if the property (or stock) depreciates below the Strike Price, so that the option is more expensive to use than purchasing the asset in the open market.

Thus, a call option is used when we feel the price of the asset (our stock) is going to appreciate in value. The call locks in a lower buy price and lets us profit nearly equal to owning the stock outright. We can then sell the stock, or contract, for nearly the difference between the strike/purchase price and the current price of the stock. For a little bit of money, you lock in at a lower buy price, which allows you to profit enormously.

The key element of a call option is that it allows an investor with a bullish forecast to lock in a purchase price for a period of time by risking a fraction of the cost of the underlying shares. In many cases, a few hundred dollars can control several thousand dollars worth of a stock. The most the investor can lose is the price paid (premium) for the option contract and the potential profit has no limit.

Few option contracts are actually exercised and the bulk of trading in the options market is simply investors buying and selling contracts prior to them expiring. It's not much different than the trading of shares of stock except that shares don't have an expiration day and option contracts do. All the movement in the price of an option contract is primarily based upon the change in price of the underlying stock and the passage of time. Think of an option contract as a "side bet" on a stock's movement.

THE PUT OPTION

- The house is valued at $200,000.

- We strike a deal (option contract) with the insurance company to insure the house for $200,000 for one year (Strike Price).

- If the house burns down anytime before the year expires, our loss is insured up to $200,000 (Date of Expiration).

- We will pay $2,000 for this policy. This fee is non-refundable whether the house burns down or not (Premium).

- The house catches fire and there is $100,000 in damage. Our policy covers the $100,000 loss (Exercise or Sell the Option).

While we use a call option for an up-trending stock, there is a different option we use to protect ourselves or profit from stocks that are falling. Returning to our example of the home, let's look at another type of option. When owning a home, what do you use to protect yourself against the asset depreciating quickly—perhaps even unexpectedly—due to fire, earthquakes, floods, and even teenagers? That's right, you take out an insurance policy where someone else assumes the risk for you. They take on the risk as long as you are willing to give something for it: a premium. For a certain amount of money, they will continue to protect your asset until the expiration date on the policy. At that time, you pay a new premium and they offer to protect you for another term.

Looking at the insurance policy, do you notice anything similar to the call option we just went over? In both instances, each contract used similar terminology. The face value of the insurance policy is actually a strike price—a price guarantee at where you can either buy or be paid something. The expiration date identifies a certain date when the contract will expire between the two parties. And the premium on each contract is the amount you pay in advance to own the contract, a non-refundable fee that obligates the seller to deliver on his promise.

> While we use a call option for an up-trending stock, there is a different option we use to profit from stocks that are falling—a put option. This is a type of insurance where someone else assumes the risk for you.

In other words, an insurance policy is actually just like a put option contract. Here's how it works.

First of all, looking back at the home example, if you insure the property for its full $200,000 value, how much is that policy really worth? Actually nothing! You see, if there is no loss, the insurance company isn't going to pay anything! And they certainly won't return the premium that you paid. That's the fee they were paid for taking the risk that your home might burn down.

On the other hand, let's say, one day while you're gone an iron is left on, face down—by one of your children, of course. Chances are good that something is going to happen during your absence that will surprise you upon your return. Let's say the house only burns halfway down—not a total loss. Fortunately, you are insured. So how much is your insurance now worth? It's worth half of the listed value on the contract—in this case, $100,000.

Now, let's say the fire department arrived late, too late to save the structure. Now how much is your policy worth? It is worth the full value listed on the contract, or $200,000. In other words, the greater the loss, the more the contract is worth. In other words, it pays to be insured!

Think about it. We use insurance policies for almost every important financial area of our lives, such as our home, cars, life, health, etc. But for one of the largest assets we may ever own, we leave it almost completely unprotected. What is it? OUR PORTFOLIOS—our retirement nest egg. How many of you have a policy to cover any loss, should something happen to it? If the market suddenly drops significantly, will it affect the value of your portfolio? Of course it will, and, quite frankly, it happens all too often. Very few people know they can protect themselves against this kind of loss. There is an option you can buy to do this for you.

PUT OPTIONS ON STOCKS:

- AAPL is currently trading at $140 per share.

- We think it's going to drop in value over the next few months.

- We buy an option contract that gives us the right to sell 100 shares of AAPL for $140 per share.

- We pay a premium of $5 per share up front, or $500 for the contract.

- The option expires in 3 months.

- On expiration day, AAPL is trading at $100 per share.

- Our contract is now worth $40 per share or $4,000 ($140 less $100).

- We can sell our contract or exercise it.

- Our profit either way is $4,000 less the $500 premium we paid for the contract or $3,500.

The kind of option contract we are going to talk about is certainly a type of insurance. When your house burns down, the insurance company says "Don't worry, we'll PUT it back." And that is actually the name of the option contract we are going to use—a PUT OPTION (remember, put back).

The put contract allows you to sell your stock at a higher price guaranteed by the option contract, even though the stock may fall to a much lower price on expiration day. In other words, if you purchase AAPL for $140 and also purchase a put contract to insure it, then if the stock drops to $100, or even lower, you're not concerned! You can use your put contract to sell that stock at anytime during the contract period for the $140 strike price, because you paid your premium.

> **The put contract allows you to sell your stock at a higher price guaranteed by the option contract, even though the stock may fall to a much lower price on expiration day.**

In that example, the stock has fallen to $100, but you can still sell the stock for $140. Thus, the contract is worth $40 per share to you—the difference between the strike price and the actual current price of the stock. The difference between the present value and the strike price is referred to as the "Equity" of the option. All you have to do to be protected is to buy that $140 put option for a small premium (perhaps just a few dollars a share) up front, and then the protection is yours for the term of the contract.

When people hear about this concept, their first question is usually, "Well, who would want to buy the stock from me, at the higher price, after it's dropped?" Actually, they may not want to buy it from you, but because they SOLD you a contract, this in essence obligates them. Remember, when you sell an option you don't already own you accept the obligation that comes with the contract, which is to buy stock if it's a call option and sell stock if it's a put option.

The next question is almost invariably, "But why would they want to sell me that kind of contract when they could lose money?" Stop to think for a minute. What are some of the wealthiest companies in the world? Insurance companies. How did they become so wealthy? By collecting premiums from millions of homeowners and investing those revenues. Sure, once in a while a house burns down and they have to pay a claim that is going to be far more than the premium they collected for that policy, but as long as they collect more premiums than they pay in claims, they continue to amass wealth. And that's what happens with the puts you purchase.

Someone is willing to assume the risk your stock might go down on the basis that you will pay them a premium, now, that they can use to invest for themselves. And guess what? Not every stock goes down. In those cases, the put option buyer does not have to buy the stocks, but can keep the premiums! In fact, you may be interested to know you can actually make money by purchasing a put contract if a stock goes down!

When buying put contracts, some people almost never own the stock they're insuring. Here's an easy way to think about this: When your house burns down, the insurance company delivers a check to you for the amount of the loss. The greater the loss, the bigger the check. Well, it's possible to insure homes you don't even own! That's right, you can insure your neighbors' homes by paying a small premium on each. Then if one or more burns down, the insurance company brings you a check for each loss!

It's exactly the same with stock. You can buy put contracts on stocks you don't own—those that you think may go down. Then, if they do, you get paid for the loss—the difference between the strike price on the contract and the actual lower price of the stock! Getting paid is a simple process: just sell back the option contract you purchased, to the market, for more than you paid for it. You see, the contract becomes more valuable the further the stock goes down. And if you pay a few dollars to own the contract, it may become worth 150 percent, 200 percent, 300 percent, or more of its original value, based on how far the stock has fallen.

Trading options is really not much more complicated than trading stocks. The mechanics of placing an order for an option is very similar to that of placing a stock order. Options contracts are traded on several major exchanges just like stocks. The largest options exchange is the Chicago Board Options Exchange.

An option trade is initiated by placing an opening order. This order can be either a buy or sell order depending on the option strategy being used. To exit an option trade, a closing order is place that is the opposite (buy or sell) of the order placed to initiate the trade.

Options are traded by the contract and a contract typically controls 100 shares of the underlying stock. Prices are quoted in per share increments. To determine the price per contract, the quote is multiplied by 100. You can determine the per contract price by simply moving the decimal point in the quote two places to the left.

There is a bid and an ask price for every option and they change constantly as the price of the underlying stock fluctuates up and down. The bid price is the price an option contract can be sold for and the ask price is the price a contract can be purchased for.

An ask price of $2.25 would indicate a contract may be purchased for $225. A bid price of $2.20 would indicate that same contract could be sold for $220. The difference between the bid and ask price is called the spread. The spread is how the market makers and exchange make their money. Think of the spread as the toll that is paid to trade the option contract. This is NOT a commission. Commissions are paid to the brokerage firm who facilitates the trade for you.

Before you can trade options, you need to complete an option agreement with your brokerage firm. This is like an account application that lists your current financial position as well as outlining your goals and objectives. Brokers use this form to determine your suitability for the many varieties of option strategies and assign you a "level" for trading. Most brokers use a scale of 1-5 for these levels.

A level one trader is approved for the most basic and conservative option strategies and a level five trader is approved for the most complex and risky strategies. You will be assigned a level based upon your experience in trading and your financial strength. You can increase your approved level as you gain more experience and increase the size of your account. If you want to be approved for a more advanced level of trading, you initiate the review process simply by asking their customer service staff to review your current trading level. Based upon the information you provide them, they will make an assessment as to which level you will be approved.

To summarize, let's review what an option is:

- An option is a contract that gives the owner the right to buy or sell a stock at a set price for a specific period of time.

- The key elements are that the price is fixed, and there is a specific time frame for the contract.

- The premium is the price that you pay for the option.

- A call option is the right to BUY stock at a set price, for a set period of time.

- A put option is the right to SELL stock at a set price, for a set period of time.

- Option contracts are traded on an exchange just like shares of stock.

- Prices are quoted in "per share" increments. Since option contracts are typically based upon 100 shares of stock, the price of the contract is the quoted price multiplied by 100. For example a quote of $2.25 would indicate the current price per contract for that option is $225.

- All quotes include a bid and ask price. The bid price is the current price an option contract can be sold for and the ask price is the current price for which an option contract can be purchased.

REVIEW

1. If you sell an option, you accept an *OBLIGATION*.

2. If you buy an option you have the *RIGHT* to exercise it.

3. Buying a Put option on a stock would indicate you have a *BEARISH* forecast for that stock.

4. A *PUT* option could be used to insure a stock or portfolio.

5. The price you pay for an option contract is called the *PREMIUM*.

FOR ANSWERS GO TO: WWW.TRADERSLIBRARY.COM/TLECORNER

CHAPTER 6

CALL OPTION STRATEGIES

COVERED CALLS ON STOCKS

Our first strategy is a "Covered Call." This is a powerful income-producing strategy that helps you generate immediate cash flow from the stocks you own. This is an excellent strategy to start with if you're new to options because it is so conservative. The covered call strategy is actually less risky than owning stock outright because you collect a premium that provides a little insurance against a drop in the price of the stock. You only need to be approved for level one trading to do the covered call strategy, and most brokerage firms will allow you to do this strategy in a retirement account, like an IRA.

When it comes right down to it, there are really only three ways to make money on a stock:

1. Buy the shares and hope to sell them at a later date at a higher price than you paid for them.

2. Collect a dividend that is paid quarterly by many public companies. The problem here is that many companies don't pay dividends and the actual dividend yield for those that do is often very small; so it's not the primary motivation to buy a stock.

3. Sell options on the stocks you own to generate consistent and reliable income from them regardless of whether they are going up, down, or sideways.

This third way to make money with stocks is probably the least understood and, in my opinion, the most powerful and consistent. The fact is that most investors I've taught in my seminars over the years are amazed when they learn this strategy. Most comment that they never knew you could generate income from stocks you own and many wonder why their broker or financial advisor never told them about this strategy. The truth is that most simply don't understand it, so they never recommend it.

I think this strategy is a great way to learn the concepts of options because it is so forgiving. In this strategy, we put time on our side, unlike buying an option where time is our enemy. This will allow us a lot of flexibility. You can be a little bit wrong in your forecast for the stock and still potentially make a profit with the covered call strategy. You cannot say that about many strategies in the investment world, but you can about this one.

To help you understand the concept behind the covered call strategy, think back to the example of the homeowner who entered into the lease with the option to buy. He owned the home and was able to generate $5,000 in immediate income by giving your friend the right to buy the home for $100,000 during the next two years. He basically sold a call option to your friend that allowed him to "call away" his home at anytime during the term of this contract for $100,000. Since he owned the house, he was "covered" in that he would be able to fulfill his obligation to deliver the house to the buyer for $100,000, regardless of the price of the house at the time. This homeowner did what is called a "Covered Call" in the options world, and it's one of my favorite option strategies.

We use this same approach in the stock market to generate income on optionable stocks we own. When doing a covered call, we sell, to another investor, the right to buy our stock for a predetermined price. This is a transaction with an investor we will never know or meet. We get paid in advance, but tie up our stock for the term of the contract. If the stock doesn't rise past the price we agreed to in the contract, we get to keep our stock because the predetermined price is higher than market, and not a good deal. If it goes above the strike price of our contract, we have to sell it because the guaranteed price is now lower than the market, and a good deal for the investor with whom we struck the deal.

The foundation of covered calls is that you must own stock. If you sell an investor the right to buy stock from you that you don't already own, you have unlimited risk. If the stock goes $100 above the price you agreed to in your contract, you have to go into the market and buy the stock, only to turn around and sell it for the lower price to which you agreed. This is called a "Naked Call" because you did not own the stock to "cover" your obligation.

Covered call selling is one of the most conservative option strategies. In fact, it's the only option strategy that most brokers allow you to do in a retirement account. It's also a very powerful income strategy that most investors simply don't understand. The best part about this strategy is that we don't have to find another investor to buy the call options we want to sell. The market finds someone for us. We simply have to say we want to do it and place the order. Isn't America great?

> Covered call selling is one of the most conservative option strategies. In fact, it's the only option strategy that most brokers allow you to do in a retirement account. This powerful strategy can also generate immediate cash flow from the stock you own—regardless of market trend.

Let's look at how you can begin to take advantage of this powerful strategy and generate immediate cash flow from the stock you own—regardless of the market trend.

WHAT ARE THE RISKS?

- **Overall Risk is Less than Owning Stock**

    Selling covered calls is actually less risky than owning stock because you create some income that provides a small cushion against a decline in the value of the stock. It's like someone paying rent on a house you own.

- **Opportunity Risk or Potential Missed Profits**

    A more subtle risk associated with this strategy is the opportunity risk. When you sell a covered call, you agree to sell your stock at a set price. That, in effect, puts a ceiling on your potential profits. If the stock goes above that price, you cannot participate. The person who bought the call option from you earns that profit. Your profit is limited to the strike price of the contract, plus the premium you were paid to enter into the covered call play. And, since option trades settle in one day, unlike stock trades that take three days, the income hits your account the day after you sell a call option.

You may feel badly about missed profits if you have given someone the right to buy your stock for $40 per share by selling them a call option, only to see the stock go to $50 by the expiration day. But, like we said earlier, lost opportunity is much easier to take than lost money.

WHAT ARE THE BENEFITS?

- **Generate Monthly Cash Flow from Stocks You Own**

    The appeal of covered calls is the income. If you own stocks with options, you have the potential to generate a paycheck from that stock every month for the rest of your life. This is a powerful principle that is understood by very few investors.

- **Downside Protection**

    The income from selling call options gives you a bit of downside protection on your stock in the event of a sudden decline in the value.

- **Ride out the Dips**

   This income also provides an easy way to ride out the dips that all stocks make from time to time.

THREE WAYS TO USE COVERED CALLS

BUY—WRITE

When you see the word "write" associated with option investing, it implies you are "selling" options, as is the case with a covered call. This is the approach you might use if you don't already own a stock that would allow you to do covered calls. You could identify an optionable stock, go into the market and buy some shares, and then immediately sell call options against those shares to create income. Those who use this approach are not trying to make money on the purchase and subsequent sale of the stock, but are trying to create a reasonable return from the income on the options alone. An ideal buy/write play may result in a wash on the stock, but the income from the call options provides a profit, from a slight percentage to as much as 15 percent on the total money invested in the stock, in as little as a month. This is a conservative approach to covered calls.

For example, we find a stock that is trading for $20 per share and the $20 call option is selling for $2. We go into the market and buy 100 shares of the stock for $2,000, and then immediately sell one contract of the $20 call and collect $200 the next day. We have given someone the right to buy the stock we own for the same price we paid for it. If the stock is above $20 on the expiration day, they will buy our stock. We get back our $2,000, and also keep the entire $200 we collected from selling the call option. We now have $2,200 in cash in our account. We've made a 10 percent return that month and can begin looking for another stock with which we can do it all again.

LEGGING IN

This is a more aggressive approach to covered calls that involves looking for stocks that are trending up and then buying them to hold while they rise. Stocks that have the green, or up, arrows we've learned about are good candidates for "legging in." After you purchase the stock, you hold it until you see that it is beginning to slow down. This may be indicated by the peaking of the MACD or red, or down, arrows on any of the indicators. At that moment, sell a call option and collect the income. By waiting while the stock is still rising, the investor is able to earn more profit on the stock, and the income is simply added on. The risk involved in legging in is that far too often you buy a stock in hopes that it will rise so you can sell a covered call, and instead it goes down in price. Now you own a stock that has fallen in value and the income you could have earned by selling the call options is not enough to offset your loss.

For an example of how legging in works, we buy XYZ stock just as it is breaking out, as indicated by the green, or up, arrows. We pay $20 per share for 100 shares. We hold the stock for a week and it rises to $25. It looks as if it will continue to rise. We see that the $30 call option is selling for $1, so we sell one contract and collect $100. The stock continues to rise and on expiration day it is at $32, $2 higher than the strike price of the call option we sold.

The owner of the call option exercises his/her right to buy our 100 shares for $30 as we agreed. Since we paid only $20 for this stock, we have earned a $10 per share profit. But that's not all; we also earned another $1 from the income on the call option, making our profit $11 per share, or $1,100. We earned all the profit between our purchase price and the strike price of the call option we sold, plus the income from the covered call.

EXIT STRATEGY

Some investors like to use the covered call strategy to exit a stock position they think has little potential of continuing to rise. They do this by selling a call option with a strike price just below the current price of the stock. This increases the probability that the person who bought this call option will exercise their right to buy this stock at the strike price. But since the strike price is lower than the current price of the stock, the call buyer is going to have to pay the stockowner a larger premium for this right. This larger premium makes up for the small discount the stock owner is giving the call option buyer, and usually allows them to make a bit more than the strike price on the sale of their stock.

For example, let's say you bought some AOL stock a year ago for $50 and it's now trading for $78. Based upon your analysis of the stock, you feel it won't be going up much more from here, but you're hesitant to sell it now because you don't want to miss out if it moves higher.

We decide to sell a call option with a strike price of $75 ($3 below the current price of AOL) because we can collect $6 per share (the premium for the call option). Now, if the stock remains anywhere above $75 on expiration day, you are obligated to sell your stock for $75. However, with the additional $6 you collected from the call option, your actual selling price is $81. The best part is that you get $81 even if the stock drops to $75 from $78 because you are going to get "called out" of your stock at any price above $75. You earn an extra $6 by selling the call option you might not have earned if you had held onto your stock.

SELECTING A STOCK FOR A COVERED CALL

MUST-HAVE OPTIONS

In order to do the covered call strategy on a stock, the stock must have options available.

$10 TO $50 PRICE RANGE

Stocks in the $10 to $50 price range generally offer some of the best potential returns. The reason for this is that the price of a call option is not necessarily tied to the price of the underlying stock. In other words, the at-the-money call option for a $20 stock may be trading at $2, which represents a 10 percent potential return on the income from the call. By contrast, the at-the-money call option for a $100 stock may only be trading for $4, which represents only a 4 percent potential return from the income. Since you must own the stock to do the covered call strategy, buying more expensive stocks often makes it difficult to get the same potential returns as you can get with lower-priced stocks. This is not to imply that it's impossible to get a decent rate of return doing covered calls on higher-priced stocks. It's just that it is rarer. The most notable exceptions are very volatile stocks like technology and Internet companies where the options are extremely expensive and offer comparable potential returns.

A word of caution: just because you can get the same potential rate of return on a high-priced stock doesn't mean it is conservative. Be sure to factor in the added volatility of the stock and determine if the stock is suitable for you to own considering your tolerance for risk.

MINIMUM 3 TO 5 PERCENT POTENTIAL MONTHLY RETURN

We suggest only considering stocks for covered calls with a minimum potential return of 3 to 5 percent per month, or better. This is not to say that if you can't get 5 percent you shouldn't do covered calls. If you already own a stock and would like to do covered calls on it, the best potential return you can get is 2 to 3 percent, and that's better than nothing. The point to understand is that if you're looking to invest new money in a stock to do covered calls, limit your prospects to those stocks that offer, at the very least, a modest rate of return. The covered call report tool, on the toolbox, screens potential candidates to find only those stocks that offer a minimum 5 percent monthly return, or better, from the call income.

MINIMUM OPEN INTEREST OF 50 CONTRACTS

Try to avoid doing covered calls with options that have little or no open interest. Open interest is a key indicator of activity in an option contract. Liquidity is better the higher the open interest is in an option contract. This usually translates to tighter spreads and fairer prices. The option interest for each contract is usually displayed on the option quote chain along with the current bid and ask prices. Contracts with low open interest generally have wide price spreads between the bid and the ask, and might be difficult to sell at a fair price. We suggest avoiding contracts with less than 50 contracts of open interest. If you insist on selling a contract with less than 50 contracts of open interest, use a limit order on the call to make sure you get a fair price.

To enter a covered call trade, you must first own the stock you are planning to play. You must own 100 shares of stock for each call option you sell. For example, if you own 500 shares of XYZ stock you could sell five call options on XYZ. You do not have to sell five, but that is the maximum you could sell and still be covered. Since selling a call option carries with it the obligation to sell 100 shares of the underlying stock at the strike price of the contract, owning 100 shares of the underlying stock assures that you will be able to meet that obligation should the circumstances require it; thus you can "cover" your obligation. That's where the strategy gets its name.

You sell a covered call by placing a "sell to open" order for the contract with the strike price you have selected. Think of the strike price as the price at which you are willing to sell your stock. The closer the strike price to the current price of the stock, the higher the premium that you will collect for selling the call option. The higher the strike price you select, the less the premium. You can also select the expiration month for your call option. That is the date that the buyer of the call option has to decide whether to exercise their right to buy your stock or not. Quite simply, they will only exercise that right if the strike price of the call option they bought is less than the current price of the stock in the open market.

On expiration day if the stock is higher than the strike price of your covered call, your stock will be called away. This is all handled automatically by your broker. Your shares are sold at the strike price of the call and the cash is deposited in your account. The obligation to sell stock has been fulfilled. You also get to keep the premium you collected at the time you entered the covered call trade. So your net return is the selling price of the stock plus the premium you collected from the option contracts. You are now free to use that money for whatever you wish. You can find another stock to purchase and do it all over again.

If the stock is below the strike price of the covered call on expiration day, you will be able to keep your stock, which would be worth the current price as quoted in the market. You would also keep the premium you collected when you entered the covered call trade. Once expiration day passes, the obligation associated with the call option expires, and you are free to choose another option to sell for a future expiration month in return for another premium.

If the stock has dropped while you had the covered call position in place, you are still at risk of losing money. The premium collected will provide a small amount of downside protection; but, if the stock should drop farther than the amount you collected in premium, you will be losing some of your initial investment. This is the primary risk of a covered call trade—stock ownership. The positive thing is that you have a small amount of insurance from the premium you collect from the covered call that you would not have if you didn't employ the covered call strategy. That's why I like to say that doing covered calls is less risky than just buying stock and doing nothing.

You can close out a covered call trade anytime prior to expiration by first buying to close the covered call position. This trade will offset the trade you placed to enter the covered call trade and remove the obligation to sell stock. Once you have closed out the covered call position, you are free to sell your stock if you choose. If you don't close the covered call position first before selling your stock, you will create a "naked call" position. This is one of the riskiest option trades you could make and one that is only allowed for the most sophisticated and financially strong investors. The reason this is the case is because you still have the obligation to sell stock by virtue of the call option contract you sold and now you no longer have the shares to "cover" that obligation. Should the call option be exercised, you would have to buy stock in the open market, perhaps at a much higher price and then turn around and sell it at the strike price of your covered call to fulfill the obligation. Fortunately, most brokerage firms employ sophisticated systems that keep investors from ever getting into a naked position.

REVIEW

1. Selling a call option on a stock you do not own is called a
   COVERED call option.

2. When doing a covered call, you still have the risk of the stock dropping in value. What is the other primary risk of the covered call strategy? *MISSED upside OPPORTUNITY*

3. Buying shares of stock and simultaneously selling call options on the same stock is known as a *BUY + WRITE*

4. The primary goal of using the covered call strategy is to generate *MONTHLY INCOME*

5. If the stock price is above the strike price of the call option you sold on expiration day, your stock will be *CALLED AWAY*

FOR ANSWERS GO TO: WWW.TRADERSLIBRARY.COM/TLECORNER

CHAPTER 7

PUT OPTION STRATEGIES

In this chapter I'd like to help you understand how to use put options to protect your portfolio and to profit from falling stock prices.

A put option, as we noted earlier, is the right to sell stock at a set price for a set period of time. In a sense, buying a put option contract locks in a selling price (the strike price of the put) for 100 shares of the underlying stock. The seller of the put must honor that price; no matter how much lower the price of the stock is at expiration.

It's important that you understand that you don't need to actually own shares of the underlying stock to buy a put on that stock. You can buy a put on any optionable stock and profit if the price of the stock drops below the strike price of that put.

As I mentioned before, the two primary uses of put options are to insure your stocks against falling prices and to profit from falling prices on stocks you don't own. The first strategy is to use a put option as an insurance policy. We call this a "protective put" on stocks we already own.

The second reason to use put options is to profit or to speculate on falling prices for stocks or indexes—or whatever investment vehicle we are using.

BUYING PUT OPTIONS

- Protective puts (insurance policy)

- Speculating on falling prices

Above are the two primary ways to use puts. I think it is very important for you to understand that you can use an option to protect yourself. This is the primary reason options were created in the first place. They were created to be used as hedges—to protect an investment portfolio against losses or unexpected movements.

Mutual fund managers and other professionals understand the importance of hedging against losses. They look to the options market during times of high market volatility to inexpensively insure their portfolios against the unexpected. These very same tools and strategies the professionals use to insure their portfolios are available to the individual investor who understands how to use them properly.

So let's take a close look at these; let's break them down and give you some of the tools and resources you need to use puts effectively to either protect yourself in a bear market or to speculate on falling prices.

PROTECTIVE PUT STRATEGIES

First, we're going to look at how to use puts for protection and then we will look at how you can use them as a vehicle to profit from falling stock prices.

We like to relate option trading to real estate because most investors are homeowners, or prospective homeowners, and have a basic grasp of the elements of a simple real estate transaction.

We use an example of a young couple buying their first house using a lease with an option to buy. We assume that the market value of the house goes up during the term of their option and they eventually exercise their right to buy the house at the agreed upon price in their contract. Now they are the proud owners of a home valued at $200,000 in the current market.

I want you to put yourself in this young couple's position. If you're a homeowner, think of the current value of your home. A home is one of the largest investments most people make in their lives and therefore, most homeowners—especially those who have a mortgage—hedge themselves to protect their investment.

Let's use our example of a house worth $200,000. Our objective is to protect and preserve our investment in that house. The traditional way to do this is by purchasing a homeowner's insurance policy.

Put Options

House is worth $200,000

We strike a deal (option contract) for someone to insure the house for $200,000 for a year

Strike Price

If the house burns down anytime before the year expires, our loss is covered up to $200,000

Date of expiration

We will pay $2,000 for this policy. We do not get it back whether the house burns down or not

Premium

The purpose of an insurance policy is to protect us against events that could cause damage to our home and reduce its value or destroy it completely. This includes things like a hurricane, or a flood, or a fire, or a tornado. Any of these disasters can cause significant damage to your home. If your home were damaged by one of these catastrophes, you would make a claim to the insurance company and they would cover the cost of "putting" your house back to its original condition, as long as the costs were within the predefined limits of your policy. None of this should be too surprising to those of you who have a homeowner's insurance policy. Insurance is one of life's necessary evils.

What you may not realize is that an insurance policy has many of the same features as a put option contract. First of all, a policy is basically a contract between you and the insurance company. The face value of the policy is just like the strike price of an option contract. And, just as with insurance, there is a specified time in every policy when it expires and we need to pay a premium to keep the policy in force. Hopefully, this is starting to sound familiar.

To summarize, an insurance policy has a strike price, expiration day, and premium—just like an option contract. As is the case with an option, the seller of a policy is bound by the terms of the contract and has the obligation to perform in the event of a claim.

An insurance policy is just like a put option because its value increases as the asset it is protecting drops in value. Let's go back to our example of the $200,000 house. Let's say you leave your teenagers at home one day and they happen to leave the iron on, face down. The house catches fire and there is $50,000 done in damage. The insurance policy is now worth $50,000 because that's what the insurance company would be obligated to pay on the claim. You would not get your premium back, and you would have to deduct that from the insurance claim to figure your net benefit.

Put Options

House goes down in value to $150,000

We strike a deal (option contract) for someone to insure the house for $200,000 for a year

Strike Price

If the house burns down anytime before the year expires, our loss is covered up to $200,000

Date of expiration

We will pay $2,000 for this policy. We do not get it back whether the house burns down or not

Premium

House catches fire and there is $50,000 in damage. Our policy covers the $50,000 loss

Exercise or Sell the Option

When you buy a put option, you're basically insuring a stock against a fall in price below the strike price of the put you buy. If the stock is lower than that price on expiration day, you can offset the loss in your stock with the profits on your put option. Your profit is the difference between the strike price of the put and the current price of the stock.

If you bought a $70 put option on Cisco for $2 ($200 per contract) and the stock was trading for $65 on expiration day, your put would be worth $5, or $500 per contract, less the $2 premium you paid for the option for a net profit of $3, or $300 per contract.

BUYING PEACE OF MIND

It's important that you understand that just like with insurance, the premium you pay for an option is non-refundable and must be considered a cost that needs to be deducted from your profits. Another thing to consider is that even if your house doesn't burn down, the insurance company will not give you back your premium. It works the same with the option. The premium you pay for the option is your maximum loss if the stock doesn't move in the direction you need it to go.

Now let's turn the table a little and look at this transaction from the perspective of the insurance company. When they issue a policy, they accept the risk of paying up to the face value of the house if it burns to the ground. That's a huge risk for such a small premium. What's their motivation to take such a big risk? They know there is only a small chance your house will burn down; and considering all the homes they insure, they will easily collect enough premiums to pay those few claims and still have some profit left over.

It's a numbers game they play. Now, obviously, it works for them. If you're like me, when you travel to large cities, you can look at the skylines and pick out some of the biggest buildings. It is amazing to see how many of those big buildings have insurance company names on them.

The model definitely works. In essence, they sell the option, collect the premiums, and if the house doesn't burn down, they get to keep it. Also, they know that the majority of people will pay the premiums their entire life, and only a small percentage of those people will ever need to make a claim against that policy. What insurance companies basically do is sell puts. It's a great income strategy—as long as there are no "wildfires" or "hurricanes."

Now all of this doesn't mean we don't want to have insurance. As a homeowner, we shouldn't look at it and think, "Since our house didn't burn down, we don't get anything from our insurance." It gives us peace of mind. It enables us to sleep at night—just knowing that we are insured.

> An insurance policy has a strike price, expiration day, and premium—just like an option contract. As is the case with an option, the seller of a policy is bound by the terms of the contract and has the obligation to perform in the event of a claim.

Do you see how this all works out? That is the beauty of a put option. It's very similar in nature to an insurance policy. The biggest difference when we apply this analogy to stocks is that you don't need to own the house to buy a policy on it. Imagine having a policy on each house in the neighborhood you live in. If one of your neighbor's homes burned down, the insurance company would bring the check to your house. Just the same, you don't need to own a stock to buy a put.

That's the next aspect of put options we're going to look at, buying puts for profits. But first, let's make sure we understand how to use them for protection.

PROTECTIVE PUTS

To review, each contract protects 100 shares. In addition, protective puts:

- Lock in a selling price (strike price).
- Must be closed out on, or before, the expiration day.
- Offset loss from strike price to current price.
- Can be bought back if it is no longer needed.

Now, mentally replace the house in the previous example with stock. This could be individual stock you've owned or maybe even stock you own right now. Think about some of the stock you have in your portfolio right now. Let's look at how you might be able to protect it. If you don't want to incur any more substantial losses during a bear market, you might consider put options on those stocks that have you worried.

Keeping in mind that we are going to replace the house in the previous example with stock should help you keep things straight. All of the terms relating to an insurance policy, as you saw here, also apply to a put option.

Each Contract Protects 100 Shares

Since put option contracts are based on 100 shares of stock, you need to buy one put for each 100 shares of stock you own to be fully insured. If you have an odd number of shares, you have to decide to either insure more or leave some uninsured as this only works in 100 share multiples.

Lock in a Selling Price (Strike Price)

You also need to determine which strike price to select for your put. You have some discretion here, but I advise you to stay with a strike price that is close to the current price of the stock. I usually like to go with the first strike price below the current price of the stock. Let's look at an example.

Let's say you own 100 shares of Amazon (AMZN) trading at $70 per share and you are worried that the company might miss their next earnings estimate. You want to insure yourself against a decline in the stock if they do, so you purchase puts. When you look at the available put option contracts for the current month, you see the closest ones are the $70 and $65 contracts. The higher the strike price of the put, the more expensive it is. This works much like choosing a deductible for an auto insurance policy. You decide where you want the insurance company to pick up the cost. The more risk you're willing to accept before the policy kicks in, the less the policy will cost. The key is that the choice is yours. It works the same way with options. You choose the strike price of the put you'd like buy, and thus you determine the amount of risk you're willing to accept before the put option protection kicks in. The premium you pay will be less the lower strike price you choose for your protective put.

Must Be Closed Out On, or Before, the Expiration Day

The other thing that impacts the premium you pay for your put is the time until expiration. The longer until expiration, the more expensive the option is. I recommend going out two to three months for protective puts. This reduces the impact of time decay on your premium and gives you more solid protection. This works just like home or auto insurance policies where they are more expensive the longer the term of the policy.

Offset Loss from Strike Price to Current Price

In this example, let's assume you chose the $65 contract that expires in two months for your insurance. Let's say the premium at the time is $2, or $200 per contract. Now you are insured against any decline in AMZN beyond $65 from today until the expiration day of that option. The difference between the current price of AMZN ($70) and the strike price of your protective put is basically your deductible. I also like to include the cost of the put because that will not be returned to me no matter what the outcome of the trade, and so it must also be considered a cost for the protection the put provides. Let's see how the protective put will reduce your loss on a drop in the stock to $60.

AMZN DROPS FROM $70 TO $60

Original price of stock	$70
Current price of stock	$60
Loss on stock	$10
Gain from $65 put option	$5
Net loss	$5 (plus $2 premium)

Once you reach the point where you've covered the deductible and the premium paid for the put option, the contract will provide dollar-for-dollar protection on any further decline in the stock.

Look at the results of the same play if the stock continues to drop lower. Notice that although the stock drops another $10, the net loss is exactly the same.

AMZN DROPS FROM $70 TO $50	
Original price of stock	$70
Current price of stock	$50
Potential Loss	$20
Gain from $65 put option	$5
Net loss	$5 (plus $2 premium)

Let's go back to the insurance example to understand another important point. You can select the deductible for your policy when you buy it, which can have a dramatic impact on your premium. It's no different with protective puts. The difference between the price of the stock and the strike price of your protective put is just like your deductible. You have to assume that loss before the policy kicks in and covers anything beyond that. The larger the deductible is (lower put strike price), the cheaper the premium.

In the AMZN example above, you could have selected the $70 put and paid a higher premium to have insurance in place for every dollar the stock dropped below the strike price. In this example, that would have offered 100 percent protection aside from the premium you paid for the option.

Can Be Bought Back If It Is No Longer Needed

The biggest difference between protective puts and insurance policies is that you can buy back the protective puts once you don't need them anymore. If you decide you only need insurance until the earnings on AMZN come out, then as soon as the news is out, you can close out the put by selling it in the option market at the current price. This will help you recoup some of your premium. With protective puts, you only need pay for what insurance you use. It's a great benefit.

After you buy a protective put, the premium fluctuates with the movement of the stock and the passing of time. The premium naturally shrinks with the passing of time, but falls faster if the stock falls in price. If the stock rises, the value of a put goes down. You can monitor the current price on the Internet to see what you can recoup anytime before expiration.

If you hold the option until expiration, you have the right to "PUT" 100 shares for each contract you own to another investor and be paid the strike price of the put for your stock. If you "exercise" your put option, that's exactly what will happen. Most brokers do this automatically if the stock is lower than the strike price of the protective put. If you don't want to sell your stock, you need to sell the put in the market some time prior to the end of trading on expiration day. The proceeds will help you offset the loss you will have on your stock position, but allow you to retain the stock to sell at a later date.

If you use protective puts as insurance, you may even find yourself wishing your stock would fall because you know you're insured. About the worst case scenario is that you buy a protective put and the stock goes up or stays the same. You'll lose the premium you paid, which will, in a sense, increase your cost basis on the stock. But if it means you will sleep better at night, it's worth it. It's no different than insuring your house and not having it burn down. You don't get your premium back, but at least you have peace of mind.

> **You can use protective puts on an entire portfolio just as easily as on individual stocks.**

The final thing I want to mention before we move on to "Puts for Profit" is that you can use protective puts on an entire portfolio just as easily as on individual stocks. Since many indexes have options traded on them, you can use these puts as insurance on a basket or portfolio of stocks. The NASDAQ Exchange Trade Fund shares, the QQQQ, has options that offer a simple way to hedge a technology-heavy portfolio. This is just another thing to consider when you feel insurance is needed.

KEY POINTS ABOUT PROTECTIVE PUTS

So let's summarize what we've learned about protective puts.

Buy Protective Puts 2 to 3 Months Away from Expiration

The first key point is to buy a little bit of time. Options are like ice cubes— always melting. The closer an option gets to expiration, the faster it melts. So it's important for you to understand that by going out to future months for your insurance, you are subjecting yourself a little less to the natural decay of time that takes place with any option. It will cost you a little more money, but it's usually money well spent. Remember, the fastest time decay is taking place in that last month right before expiration.

This is especially true if you only intend to hold the protective put for a short time. Buying the shortest term option saves you a little money upfront, but it doesn't allow you the luxury of changing your mind without incurring another commission and buying more time in a new put option. The time value as it decays going forward will have less of an impact on your positions than if you had bought the two or three-week period. So generally, look at going out two to three months. You can certainly go out longer, but that's up to you to decide based on your individual forecast and how long you want to be protected with this protective put.

Buy Out-of-the-Money Puts—This is Your Deductible

Usually you want to buy out-of-the-money puts. This basically means you want to buy put options that are lower than the current price of the stock. Give yourself a little deductible; be willing to take a little bit of risk in the stock declining in value from its present price.

I like to go to the next strike price below the current price of the stock. If I'm really worried about a drop and want to fully insure myself, I may buy the at-the-money put option.

By selecting an out-of-the-money put, you lower the cost of the insurance policy. Remember, the further down you go from the current price, the more your protective put becomes like catastrophic insurance. The premium is small, but the coverage only kicks in if there is a tremendous sell-off in the stock. It's like having a big deductible to pay before the coverage kicks in. These are decisions you have to make based on your personal forecast for the individual stocks you play.

Sell the Put before Expiration—Recover Some of the Premium

Next, we don't need to hold a protective put until expiration day if we no longer need the insurance. And if we don't need the insurance anymore, we can sell the put before it expires (as long as it's no longer needed), and recover a small portion of our premium. The longer you wait, the less the option is going to be worth. If you wait until a day or two before expiration to cash it in, don't be surprised if it is worth hardly anything. It may not even be worth enough to cover the cost of commission to sell. In that case, you may as well let it expire just in case there is a dramatic drop right before expiration day.

If you need insurance for a few days only—like to protect yourself from what could happen after an earnings announcement comes out—just buy the protective put before the announcement, and sell it after you've had a chance to see how the announcement impacts the stock. If the stock price drops dramatically, you know you're protected. If it doesn't move at all, or moves up, simply sell your put option and recover part of your premium.

Don't be surprised if the premium shrinks very quickly after an earnings announcement. Volatility is a key component of an option's price, and volatility is at its peak during times like these—when many investors are speculating on the earnings release. As soon as the earnings announcement is out, the volatility often collapses, no matter which direction the stock goes. This almost instantly reduces the premiums on the options for that stock, including the put options. So move quick if you decide you want to get out of your protective put.

Exercise the Put If You Want to Actually Sell Shares You Own

Finally, if you hold your protective put until expiration day, and see that the stock is now lower than your strike price, you need to take some action if you do not want to sell your stock. If you feel the bad times are over for this stock and now you want to hold it for an upward run, you need to close out your put by selling it, on, or before, the close of trading on expiration day. Any profit from the sale of the protective put will help to offset the paper loss on your stock. Then, you'll be back in the black that much sooner if the stock really does take off again.

BUYING PUTS FOR PROFIT

Now let's look at how to use puts to profit in a falling market.

At the beginning of this chapter I said that you do not have to own the stock to buy a put option on it. That being the case, investors wishing to profit from falling stock prices are always on the lookout for weak stocks that have the potential to fall. Unfortunately, many of us need only look to our own portfolio to find these kinds of stocks in abundance.

You can literally buy a put option on any stock with options listed. You will profit if that stock falls below the strike price of the put option you buy, on, or before, expiration day.

As I mentioned previously, this approach to put options is kind of like buying insurance on your neighbor's house, and hoping it burns down so the insurance company will bring the check to your door. Now obviously, it's a bit morbid to talk about your neighbor's house burning down, but it's an effective way to get you thinking in the right direction.

Let's look at some of the situations that create put-buying opportunities. We're going to look at each of these in some detail and then look at a few actual examples.

The first thing to consider before buying puts for profit is the trend. It may not sound right, but even in a bear market, the trend is our friend. Knowing what the current trend is will help you determine what investment strategies to consider. When is the best time to buy puts for profit? Obviously, you're going to consider buying puts for profit when the trend of the market, the major sectors, and the stock you are considering playing are down. So what's the best way to determine that?

> **The best ways to determine if the trend is down are:**
>
> • **Sector Selection**
>
> • **MACD Histogram**
>
> • **Moving Average Failures**
>
> • **Volume Analysis**
>
> • **Earning Effect**

Sector Selection

I like to do a quick check of the major market sectors using the S&P SPDR Sector Funds I discussed in chapter three to check the trends of the market and major sectors before looking for individual stocks. Simply bring them up in any charting program and apply a 21-day exponential moving averages on a one-year graph.

Try to find sectors where the index is trending down. These sectors are great places to search for individual put candidates. Once you find a weak sector, you can identify the individual stocks that make up that sector or industry group to pinpoint the weakest stocks.

When I'm looking for potential plays, I look at lots of individual stock charts and pay particular attention to the short-term moving average. If I find one that is pointing down, it becomes a candidate for further analysis.

Trying to find good put plays in a bull market is like trying to find good call plays in a bear market. It's a lot like trying to find a needle in a haystack. For those of you who tried to play call options during the last six months of 2000, you know how difficult this is. Remember, the trend is your friend, so choose strategies that profit in the prevailing trend. When the trend is down, consider buying puts or just stay on the sidelines.

MACD Histogram

In my seminars, I teach investors to recognize the first sign of weakness in a stock as the exit point for their call option plays. It's this same point that makes a great entry point for a put play. I like to use a Moving Average Convergence Divergence (MACD) histogram to help me spot weakness.

I like to think of the MACD histogram as an indicator that shows the mountains and valleys of a stock. When you buy call options, you should try to time your entry into the position to coincide with the beginning of a new mountain. The ideal exit point is the peak of that mountain. It's very difficult to get out at the very peak, so I tell my students to try to exit as close to the top of the peak as possible.

When buying puts, we want to enter our position just as the stock is beginning to show weakness. Using the MACD histogram, that would also be at or near the peak that is formed when the stock is running up. As the MACD begins to

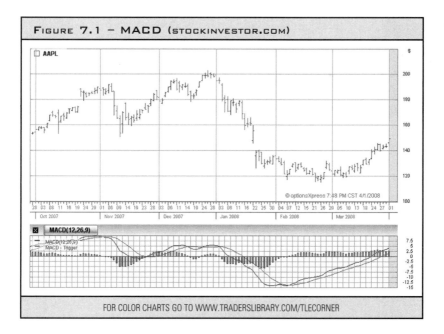

FIGURE 7.1 – MACD (STOCKINVESTOR.COM)

FOR COLOR CHARTS GO TO WWW.TRADERSLIBRARY.COM/TLECORNER

head down, the stock is usually losing ground, which is exactly what we need in order to profit from a put position.

The example of a MACD histogram (Figure 7.1) clearly shows these kind of peaks. Notice how the various peaks and valleys of the MACD histogram coincide with the ups and downs of the stock price above it.

Moving Average Failures

Another sign of weakness is when a weak stock rallies up to its moving average and then bounces back down. In the chapter on trends, we learned that stocks tend to bounce away from their moving average in the direction of the trend of the moving average. Most down-trending stocks stay below their short-term moving average for a large part of the downtrends. The short rallies that happen along the way only seem to get the stock back to the moving average where the stock encounters overhead resistance.

Overhead resistance is a powerful force that usually halts the rise in the stock and pushes it back down, following the trend. Just the opposite is true with a rising stock. With the stock above the moving average, each correction along

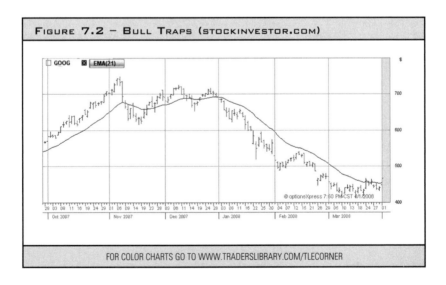

FIGURE 7.2 – BULL TRAPS (STOCKINVESTOR.COM)

FOR COLOR CHARTS GO TO WWW.TRADERSLIBRARY.COM/TLECORNER

the way takes the stock back to the moving average where it finds support. This is often where the new rally begins as the stock bounces up from this point, following the trend.

In a bullish market, the moving average is a support point where the stock tends to bounce up. In a bearish market, the moving average is a resistance point where the stock tends to bounce down. Remember the simple rule from our discussion earlier in this book on trends: stocks tend to bounce from their moving average in the direction of the trend of their moving average.

So in down-trending stocks, look for a rally toward the moving average when the stock runs out of steam and turns down. This is commonly referred to as a bull trap (Figure 7.2) because bullish investors buy into these rallies only to be disappointed when the stock hits resistance at the moving average and then breaks down again on high volume. It's at the peak of these rallies where the stock touches the down-trending moving average that we like to buy puts.

Volume Analysis

Another thing to look at is shrinking volume on upward moves. Rallies without volume lack conviction. Think of volume as "votes." The number of votes being cast for a particular stock's movement up or down is a great way to determine the strength of that move. Low volume rallies are typical in a bear market and serve as traps for the eternally optimistic bulls. It's when you see spikes in volume on the sell offs that you like to play puts. Again, this is just the opposite of everything we learned about call options and buying stock. When we're bullish, we like to see volume increase on the upward movements of the stock. When we play puts, we like to see the volume spike on the downward moves. So volume is another key indicator we follow when screening potential put candidates (Figure 7.3).

FIGURE 7.3 – VOLUME SPIKES (STOCKINVESTOR.COM)

FOR COLOR CHARTS GO TO WWW.TRADERSLIBRARY.COM/TLECORNER

Earnings Effect

Earnings announcements have become real pivot points for stocks. In a down-trending market, it takes more than just good earnings to break the trend. I am sure you have had the experience of buying a great stock on the expectation of a good earnings announcement, only to see that stock drop after the announcement came out—even though it met, or beat, the analysts' estimate. Why does this happen? I've met many investors who love to load up on call options right before an earnings announcement and then can't believe it when their calls get wiped out after a seemingly good earnings report.

You see, it's the buying that makes the stock move. If it's a widely followed stock, like Cisco or AOL, everyone is aware of the earnings dates and the bulls are positioning themselves with stocks and calls to take advantage of it. Nearly everyone who cares gets into the stock prior to the announcement. So when the announcement comes in as expected, there is no one left to buy more stock and push the price higher.

Even though the news was good, the rally runs out of steam and the stock begins to fall as some of those investors who made money on the earnings run begin to take some money off the table. I see it happen all the time.

About the only thing that can extend the earnings run is a blowout announcement that far exceeds the analysts' estimate and surprises the market. While most investors are aware of the analysts' earnings estimate, there is another number, that many on Wall Street watch, called the "whisper number." Though rarely published, this number is the real number the professionals are expecting the company to top.

This whisper number may be a few pennies higher than the analysts' estimate. A company may beat the analysts' number, and fall short of the whisper number, and get treated as if they had a poor earnings report. When you hear the news, you may think the stock will rise because they beat the estimate, but missing the whisper number results in a sell-off.

> **Earnings announcements in a bear market are a great time to play puts. If you're looking for the slight edge that tilts the scales in your favor, an earnings report might be it.**

In a bear market, just meeting the estimate is usually not enough. To overcome the tremendous pull of the downtrend, only a surprise blowout earnings report is going to get the scared investors off the sidelines to spend money on more stock. Earnings announcements in a bear market are a great time to play puts. If you're looking for the slight edge that tilts the scales in your favor, an earnings report might be it.

I am not a huge put player, but this is one time I really like to play these strategies. It feels like I have a little bit of an edge because the tendency for most stocks in a falling market is to continue to fall. There are many investors sitting there waiting for any indication of bad news in that earnings release, or in the conference call that follows. If investors sense any hesitation on the part of management, in their forecasts for the next quarter earnings report, look out below. It doesn't matter if they just reported a record quarter; the stock is going to get hammered.

If you play puts on earnings announcements in a bear market, there is a chance that the company will miss the estimate all together. This is where the big money in puts is made—and it's made very fast. One of my good friends often tells of the time when fathers took their sons to the woodshed to give them spankings when they were bad. He relates this to a stock, after the company misses an earnings estimate, "being taken to the woodshed." I think you get the picture. It's usually not pretty, unless you're holding a bunch of put option contracts—then it's like Christmas morning.

KEY POINTS ABOUT BUYING PUTS FOR PROFIT

The Trend is Your Friend

The most important thing to consider before applying any investment strategy is the trend. Let me say it for the hundredth time, "The trend is your friend." The time to play puts is when the market is weak and falling. Look for sectors and industry groups where there is weakness and identify the leaders in that group.

Only play stocks that have a down-trending moving average. Don't ever try to buck the trend by picking tops in a bull market. You may miss the first opportunity when a trend changes, but if you're following closely, then you'll certainly get the second opportunity and any others that follow.

Buy on Weakness

When buying put options for profit, you want to buy on weakness in the market, sector, and stock. Stocks that are breaking down through areas of support or turning lower from areas of resistance are the best prospects. One of the best signals is a stock bouncing lower after reaching its down-trending moving average.

Another signal that confirms weakness is peaks in the MACD histogram. This is one of the earliest signs of weakness a stock shows. Look for other indicators to follow, and to confirm the breakdown, before playing. As always; when in doubt, sit out.

Sell on Strength

Once you're in a put play, you want to monitor the individual stock and exit the play on the first sign of strength. An obvious sign would be a significant rise in the stock caused by some recent good news coming out on the company of the stock.

Stay Close to the Money

Stay close to the money when selecting your put contracts. Try to limit your selection to the at-the-money strike price—one above it or one below it. Use the price of the option to help you determine your risk. The more expensive the option, the more conservative it is. The cheaper the option, the more aggressive it is. Don't buy options just because they are cheap. The cheapest options are usually the out-of-the-money options.

I once had a wise broker tell me that if you always invest in out-of-the-money options, you'll eventually be out of money. Choose aggressive options only when you completely understand the risk and are willing to accept it.

1 to 3 Months of Time

The next key point is: one to three months of time. Most bearish moves are quick and dramatic. Thus, it makes no sense to buy options that are far from expiration when you will most likely be holding them for only a short period of time. Unless you believe the stock you're playing is headed for a long bear market, stick to contracts that are one to three months from expiration. Only choose the shortest-term options if you're certain the stock will drop by the expiration day. This may be appropriate if you're playing a potential drop on an earnings announcement that is scheduled prior to the third Friday of the current month.

I always tell my students to buy enough time, but not too much time. Remember, the longer until expiration, the more expensive the contract is.

You need to balance time and cost, and the best way to do this is by selecting a contract that best fits your forecast.

Have a Stop Loss

You should have a stop loss on a put play just like you would for any other trade. In my experience, few options that fall in price by half of what you paid for them ever recover to the purchase price, let alone produce a profit. That's why I like to use the "50 Percent Rule" as a get-out point for any option play. If the option premium falls to half of what I paid for it, I sell it and move on. Don't take it personally. You're going to have losing trades if you play options. This just means it didn't work out to your benefit this time. It's more damaging to stay in this position and watch the equity that's left melt away as the option nears expiration, than to take a loss and start looking for another good play.

If you have identified areas of support and resistance as part of your analysis of a trade, you should consider the support area as a potential exit point. Stocks often bounce off areas of support and start new upward trends. Look for areas on the chart where the stock has bounced previously. Use these areas as exit targets.

If you follow indicators, you should consider any positive breakout as an exit signal. I like to use the MACD and watch it for positive breakouts as a signal to exit a put play. It's important to remember that ignoring a sign of strength can turn a good trade bad very quickly. One of the hardest things to do is exit a losing trade. Don't hang on to puts when the stock begins to strengthen in hopes it will weaken again and allow you to exit with a profit. There will be times when a stock begins to rise after you've bought a put and it never gives you a chance to make a profit. It's the ability to take a small loss before it becomes a big one that separates the wise put players from those who lose.

Take Your Profits

The final key point: take your profits. Perhaps you've heard the saying, "You'll never go broke taking a profit." Well, it's true. Too many investors fall in love with their investments and avoid selling when they really should. Investments are vehicles for making money. When you've made some money, cash in and move on to the next investment.

After you go to all the work of finding a good trade, it just doesn't make any sense to hold on far after the first sign of weakness and give back all your paper profit. If you're going to be a successful investor, you need to learn how to take profits. It's always better to miss out on a little of the opportunity than to run the risk of giving back a profit. Leave a little profit on the table each time you trade and you'll find there is still plenty for you. We want to make sure we stay in good trades as long as the conditions allow and get out of the bad ones as quickly as possible; let our profits run and cut our losses short.

REVIEW

1. Buying a Put option on a stock you own is a form of _____.

2. **TRUE OR FALSE:** You must own a stock to buy a put option on it.

3. If you buy a Put option on a stock you don't own, you would be _____ on a drop in the price of the underlying stock.

4. The value of a Put option increases when the value of the underlying stock _____.

5. When you buy a Put option, you are in a sense locking in a _____ price for a stock.

FOR ANSWERS GO TO: WWW.TRADERSLIBRARY.COM/TLECORNER

CHAPTER 8

BEARISH CREDIT SPREADS

I've always believed that it's very difficult for any investor to forecast the direction of the market or a stock in the short term. A much easier proposition, in my opinion, is to use history and other indicators to help determine where it WON'T go. I like to call this non-directional trading and it's my personal favorite approach.

When you invest with options you are given the choice to either place the bets or take the bets. When I consider how well it works for insurance companies and casinos, I choose to take the bets, or in other words, sell options. You see, when you sell an option you put time on your side.

I like to use a simple analogy to illustrate the impact of time decay on an option. I like to think of an option as being like a cube of ice and expiration day as being a heater. Every day that passes the ice is moving closer to the heater. The ice is going to melt no matter what, but it's going to melt faster the closer it gets to the heater.

I think this little analogy puts into perspective the risk associated with options. The fact that they don't last forever makes them far riskier to buy than stock. I tell my students that when you buy an option it's not enough to be right in your forecast for the stock—you have to be right ON TIME. When you buy an option, time decay is your enemy and every day that passes is costing you money and opportunity. When you sell an option, you put time decay on your side. Time is your friend.

> **Using this non-directional approach to investing, you can win a high percentage of your trades and make great returns.**

If you can determine with a high level of probability that a stock will not move above or below a certain price range, you can create a high probability trade using options that will be profitable as long as the stock remains in that range until expiration day. Using this non-directional approach to investing, you can win a high percentage of your trades and make great returns. These types of high probability strategies won't double your money in a week, but they will help you grow your account month after month to reach your goals. I like to think of this approach to investing as the "get rich eventually" approach.

BEARISH CALL OPTION CREDIT SPREAD

This leads me to our next bear market strategy, the bearish call option credit spread. This stategy has many similarities to covered calls in the type of stocks we apply it to and in some of the basic mechanics, but the biggest difference is that we do this strategy on stocks we don't own, unlike covered calls. Here's how it works.

It all starts with finding the weakest stocks in the weakest sectors of a very weak bear market. I know some of you are already thinking this will be easy because those are the type of stocks you've been picking for years without any help whatsoever. The biggest difference this time around is that you might actually make money on them because you're now going to apply the right strategy.

A few qualities that you should look for in a stock are a clearly down-trending moving averages and high volumes of trades on the down days. The stock should always be below the down-trending moving average. It helps tremendously if there is some strong overhead resistance in the stock at a price above the current price where the stock is likely to stall if it happens to rally after you apply this strategy. Your time frame for this trade is typically just a month, so you're not going out too far in your forecast. You simply want to find a stock that nobody wants to own and you're going to sell options to other investors who are willing to place a risky bet that the stock will go up in the short term.

Now before you get too far ahead of me, let me just say that selling options is considered by many to be very risky. In fact, selling a call option is considered the riskiest of all option strategies because you're basically giving another investor the right to buy stock from you that you don't own. You're even locking in a purchase price and giving them until the expiration day of the option to decide to exercise that right or not. If they were to exercise the right of a call option, you would have to sell them stock at the agreed upon price (the strike price of the call option) no matter what the current price of the stock is.

Let's say you decide to sell a $25 call option on a stock that is currently trading for $22 and the stock rises to $30 before the option expires. You would have to buy shares in the market at $30 and turn around and sell them at $25 to fulfill the obligation of the call option you sold. There is no limit on how high a stock can go, so the risk of that strategy is considered to be unlimited. In option jargon, it's called a naked call.

It's funny that just one little difference in that scenario turns the riskiest option strategy there is into one of the most conservative. When you own the stock that you're obligating yourself to sell in our previous example, you have the ability to "cover" the obligation no matter how high the stock should rise. That's a covered call strategy and it's one of the most conservative option strategies there is.

With a bearish call spread we're going to sell a call and then use another form of insurance to cover ourselves, another call option. That's right. We're going to sell a call with a higher strike price on a stock that has been going down and then use part of the income that trade creates to buy an insurance policy in the form of another call option with a slightly higher strike price. That's

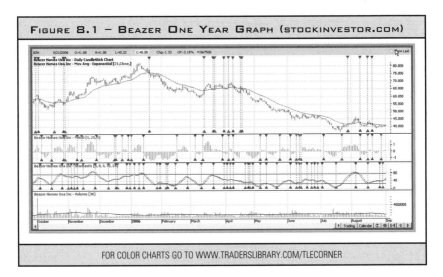

FIGURE 8.1 – BEAZER ONE YEAR GRAPH (STOCKINVESTOR.COM)

called a bear call spread, and it's a great strategy to make money by forecasting where a stock won't go.

You create the income to pay for the insurance and what's left over is your profit. Let's take a look at an example so you can see how it all works.

Figure 8.1 is a one year graph of Beazer Homes (BZH) This was one of the worst stocks from the housing sector, which was one of the weakest of 2006. Just look at that chart. It went straight down once the selling began and every rally was met with another round of selling once it hit the down-trending moving average. Just the kind of stock I love to use for the bear call credit spread.

The stock rallied back once again to the down-trending moving average on very weak volume to trade at $40 per share. This is where we expect that it will once again bounce in the direction of the moving average and head lower. We choose to sell the current month $40 call option, which is selling for $2.55 or $255 per contract, and then purchase the next call option higher, the $45 strike price, as insurance. Here's what the trade would look like based on a 1000 share position, or 10 option contracts.

STOCK CURRENTLY TRADING FOR $40 PER SHARE:

Sell the current month $40 Call for $2.55	$2550 (credit to your account)
Buy the current month $45 Call for $0.80	$800 (debit to your account)
Net income (Maximum Profit)	$1750
Maximum Potential Loss	$3250
Breakeven Point	$41.75

The maximum profit is the amount of income you collect when you initiate the trade. To calculate it, just subtract the cost of the call you buy from the income generated from the call you sold. That's the most you can make on this trade, and it's in your account the day after you place the trade. As long as the stock stays below the strike price of the call you sold, both options will expire worthless leaving you with the entire premium you collected at the beginning of this trade as a profit.

The maximum potential loss on this trade is determined by the difference in the strike price of the two option contracts used in the strategy less the net premium collected. That's the most you can lose if the stock rises substantially after you apply this strategy.

The breakeven point is determined by taking the credit you collect when you apply this strategy and adding it to the current price of the stock. Since you're collecting some income, you have that much margin for error before you start losing the money you started with.

Again, the purpose of this strategy is to pick a very weak stock and sell an option to another investor that feels the stock is going to go up and have them pay you a premium up front. As long as the stock stays the same or goes down, you win. The only way you lose is if the stock rises after you apply the strategy and even then, you have a little cushion against being wrong in the form of some income generated from the strategy. Of the three possible things that can happen to you in this strategy, two of them will result in the maximum potential profit on the trade. I like those odds.

> **Of the three possible things that can happen to you in this strategy, two of them will result in the maximum potential profit on the trade. I like those odds.**

If you use the maximum potential loss as a basis for determining your rate of return on this trade, it would result in a better than 50 percent return on the money that was at risk. You've put time on your side and you've created a trade with a limited risk and limited reward.

Let's look at what happens if the stock moves higher after you apply this strategy.

You would incur the maximum potential loss if the stock rose higher than the strike price of the call option you bought by expiration day. Once the stock rises past your breakeven point, $41.75 in this example, you begin to lose money. You can close out this trade anytime you want prior to expiration day by simply placing offsetting orders for the two options that are part of your position. The first trade would be to buy to close the option you sold (the $40 call in this example) and then to sell the option you bought to recoup any remaining premium. If the stock is really starting to rally, you could just decide to keep this option in hopes that it will continue to rise and generate a profit that could offset part of your loss on the other option. You are in control and can pull the plug on this trade anytime you want.

The bearish call credit spread strategy is a great way to make money on weak stocks in a falling market. Let's review the key points of this powerful bearish strategy.

- Stick to down-trending stocks.

- 30 to 45 day options decay fastest.

- Sell ATM or first OTM call option.

- Buy next farther OTM call option for insurance.

- Close out early if stock breaks out to the upside or if you are satisfied with the profit and want to remove risk.

I love to use non-directional strategies like the bear call spread to improve my probability of success. These are not strategies that result in windfall profits overnight, but rather create consistent solid income by putting time decay on your side while at the same time controlling risk.

In a bear market, the key to success is to stay out of the way of falling stocks. If you can do that, the bear call spread will be a consistent winning strategy for you.

— — —

REVIEW

1. Credit Spreads are a form of _____ trading.

2. A credit spread is created by _____ an option contract that is near the current price of the stock and then_____ another option contract that is a little farther away for insurance.

3. A bearish credit spread is created using _____ options and a bullish credit spread is created using _____ options.

4. Credit spreads have _____ risk and _____ reward.

5. Short term credit spreads should be created with option contracts that are _____ days from expiration.

FOR ANSWERS GO TO: WWW.TRADERSLIBRARY.COM/TLECORNER

CHAPTER 9

SHORTING STOCKS

I want to briefly mention the strategy of shorting stock. Shorting stock is a strategy that's normally used by very experienced investors to profit from declines in a stock. It's basically selling stock that you don't own, in hopes that it will drop in price so you can buy it back later at a lower price.

Selling short is basically buying low and selling high in reverse. Short sellers like to sell stock at high prices in hopes of a fall and then buy the stock to close their trade when prices are lower. As with any trade, the profit is the difference between the buying price and the selling price, less your transaction costs.

Here's a look at the points I want to address as they relate to shorting stock:

- There is unlimited risk.

- You sell stock you don't own in the hopes of buying it back later at a lower price.

- It requires a margin deposit.

- You buy low and sell high, in reverse.

The risk in short selling is substantial. You should be completely aware of the risks if you're going to consider selling stock short.

Before you're able to short stock, you need to have a margin account set up with your broker. Short selling is a difficult strategy for many investors to grasp, because it involves selling something you don't own. You see, in the stock market, you're allowed to sell stock you don't own as long as you can demonstrate your ability to buy it back later to close out the trade. You demonstrate your ability by having cash or securities in your account with a value equal to a minimum of 50 percent of the value of the stock you're selling. This is called margin and you must open a margin account with your broker in order to short sell stocks. I'll give you some additional details on margin accounts in a minute.

Let me explain what's really taking place when you place an order to sell short, and perhaps this will all make a bit more sense.

> **Shorting stock is one of the riskiest strategies there is. In fact, the risk is theoretically unlimited—there is no limit to how high the stock can go.**

Many investors get confused in that they think selling something you don't own is like selling something that doesn't exist. There is a big difference. Yes, when you sell short, you're selling stock that you don't own—but the stock must exist. It's not like you're dealing in fictitious shares.

If you don't own any shares, and you wish to sell some shares of a stock short, you must borrow the shares from another investor. Don't worry; this is something your brokerage firm does for you. You don't have to go out and find someone who owns the shares you want to sell. The broker will basically loan you the shares to sell in the market, but you need to repay the loan when you close out the trade. Closing out a short trade is called "covering." On most online broker trading systems, the trade is entered as "buy to cover" when you exit a short sell.

I know this is a little complicated, which is part of the reason most people don't short stock—they don't understand it. It's when you start doing trades you don't fully understand that you really get into trouble.

MARGIN ACCOUNT

In order to sell a stock short, you need to have, on account with your broker, margin. Margin is a deposit of cash or securities to prove that you have the ability to buy the shares needed to close the trade. Most brokers require 50 percent of the value of the stock you've shorted, and then they check the price of the stock daily to make sure you still have enough money to cover the trade. If the stock rises substantially, you may be required to add additional margin money. This is what's known as a "margin call." We'll cover that in a minute.

Think of the margin money as collateral for a loan. It's like putting up a good faith deposit. You can use cash or any marginable securities, like stocks you already own, as a margin deposit. If you have a bunch of shares of stock, or even T-bills or T-bonds, you may post them as margin.

Margin requirements do vary from firm to firm. But as a rule for most stocks, you have to put up 50 percent of the value of the stock. This is typical with most firms, although there are some that will let you go a little lower. However, some may require more than 50 percent on certain stocks they have determined to be very volatile. Check with your broker to determine their specific margin requirements before considering selling short.

Shorting stock is one of the riskiest strategies there is. In fact, the risk is theoretically unlimited. The risk you assume is anything above the price at which you sell the stock. If you short a stock for $50, you then expose yourself to the risk of $1 per share that you sold for every dollar above the $50 price. As the stock rises, you are losing money. As I said earlier, you have unlimited risk because there is no limit to how high the stock can go.

This is one of those strategies where if you're really wrong, you don't just lose money, you lose your house. Your broker may come knocking on your door and take your children. (Just kidding there.) But I mean to make the important point that shorting stock can be very risky.

SHORTING A STOCK

Let's look at how a simple short sell trade might work. Let's say you're following Yahoo! (YHOO) and that the stock is starting to show signs of weakening and the trend is starting to point down. You could use any of the signals we spoke about in the chapter on buying puts to help confirm this.

With the stock trading at $50 per share, you decide to sell short. You place an order with your broker to "sell short" 200 shares of YHOO at $50. Your account is credited with $10,000; the proceeds from the sale of 200 shares of stock at $50. You then place a protective stop order with your broker to buy to cover 200 shares at $60. When selling short, you should always have a stop.

Now you monitor the stock and see that your forecast was correct. Within a week, the stock is down $10 to $40 per share. You see the stock is getting close to a level of support, and you decide to exit your short position.

You place an order to "buy to cover" 200 shares of YHOO at $40, and a debit of $8,000 is made to your account. The difference between your purchase and sell is your profit. In this case, that's $2,000, less your transaction costs.

Let's look at the same example again and assume the stock moves against you. You get the credit for $10,000 when you enter the position. But this time, the stock begins to rise rather than fall. Within a week, the stock is up $10 from where you shorted and your stop at $60 is hit. Your order to "buy to cover" 200 shares at $60 is executed and your account is debited for $12,000.

Notice you're paying more for the stock than you originally sold it for. This means you have a loss. In this case your loss is $2,000, plus the transaction costs.

MARGIN CALL

If you short a stock and the stock begins to rise and you don't close out your position, then you may be asked by your broker to put up more collateral or margin money. This is what's known as a margin call. I like to think of it as a call from your broker telling you that you're in over your head. My advice to most is to never meet a margin call. Rather than meet the call by sending in more money, you should sell all or part of your investment to meet the margin call.

When I was in the brokerage business back in 1987, I had to make a lot of margin calls the day after "Bloody Monday." I remember going to one of the more experienced brokers that morning for a few tips on how to handle this very traumatic experience.

He said, "You simply call the customer and tell them you've got some good news and some bad news. Then tell them the good news is that one of us made money today. The bad news is that it wasn't you." You see, brokers get paid to buy and to sell, whether you've made money or not.

Investors who short stock must fully understand the risk and have the financial means to weather the storm if things turn against them. It takes great personal discipline to be a good short seller. If you let emotions take control in a short sell trade, you may lose it all before you realize it.

As you can see, it is really important to have a stop loss and to stick to it. A lot of people let this run away from them. I know of people who were shorting stock during the boom in Internet stocks. They were those wise old investors who couldn't believe that a company without any earnings could possibly keep going up. Those investors were shorting stocks like Amazon, Yahoo!, DoubleClick, and many of the other Internet stocks. It didn't matter that these companies weren't making money; investors just kept pushing these stocks up and up. Many of the stocks doubled, tripled, or quadrupled in value over short periods of time.

During this time, these so-called savvy investors were shorting the stocks. They thought it would eventually be like in the Wizard of Oz, when Toto pulled back the curtain and there

> **If you short a stock and the stock begins to rise and you don't close out your position, you may be asked by your broker to put up more collateral or margin money. This is what's known as a margin call.**

was this little old man pulling the levers and pushing the buttons—nothing like the "great and powerful Wizard" they had expected.

The problem was that these Internet stocks defied all logic and kept rising for the longest time, all the while racking up huge losses for the short sellers. Many of them met margin call after margin call, but most finally gave up and covered their short positions with substantial losses.

When the market for these stocks finally started to crumble, it was too late for many early short sellers, as they had already covered their positions. Those who were able to stay short would have been richly rewarded with huge profits from the Internet stocks collapse in 2000.

SHORTING STOCKS SUMMARY

IT'S NOT ENOUGH TO BE RIGHT

When shorting stocks, it's not enough to be right, you must be right on, or you could get wiped out. Hopefully, now, you can see that shorting stock is an extremely risky strategy and only for those savvy investors who have the financial means and personal discipline to manage those positions once they get into them.

BE READY TO TAKE FOLLOW-UP ACTION

When you short stock, you need to follow the market closely and be ready to take follow-up action or close out your position if the market moves against you. A sure sell signal is a reversal in the downward trend of the stock you're playing. Another exit signal is any jump in the price of the stock brought on by a surprise announcement of good news, or a positive signal on the technical indicators. You can use the same 10 to 20 percent stop rule for a short position that we talked about for a normal stock position in the chapter on stop loss orders.

Hopefully, this has helped you understand a little bit more about shorting stock and has maybe answered a question or two you've had about it.

Personally, I prefer to use put options to profit from falling prices, rather than to short stock. Options have a limited risk compared to the unlimited risk of short selling. The maximum potential loss on an option purchase is the premium you paid for the option. You have total control over that because you select which put option you are going to buy.

REVIEW

1. Shorting a stock has _____ risk.

2. Before you can short a stock you will need to open a _____ account at your brokerage firm.

3. The order you place to exit a short sale position is a_____ order.

4. A call from your broker to add additional cash or collateral to your account is known as a _____.

5. **TRUE OR FALSE:** You must own a stock to sell it short.

FOR ANSWERS GO TO: WWW.TRADERSLIBRARY.COM/TLECORNER

CHAPTER 10

HEDGING

The concept of hedging has been around for as long as people have been investing. Hedging was used by farmers to lock in prices for their harvest and avoid dramatic price fluctuations. We can also use hedging strategies in the stock market to protect ourselves from unexpected declines in the stocks we own. I'd like to share with you the "collar," one of the most common and popular hedging strategies for minimizing your risk in a falling market. What's nice about this strategy is that in some cases you can still have some upside potential in the stocks you own, all while totally eliminating the downside.

When all the internet companies were going public back in the last tech stock boom of the late 90's, many young computer whiz kids found themselves as instant millionaires and in some cases billionaires. Since their stocks were very volatile, many looked for ways to "lock in" their newfound wealth. Many of the big brokerage firms and investment banking companies assisted them in creating collars for their mass stock holdings. These collars assured their newfound wealth would be preserved even if the stock were to suddenly drop significantly in price. This has been a common strategy of the super wealthy, but it can work just as well for the average investor trying to protect their profits.

Before I get into the mechanics of the strategy I want to make a very important point. Hedging is just a short-term temporary solution when your stocks start to decline. Because a collar uses options, it will eventually expire and the protection will be removed. The ultimate solution to the problem of a falling stock is to sell it. Before ever considering a hedging strategy, you should first consider whether you should simply sell the stock and move to the safety of a money market account. That is the only sure way to avoid any additional losses on your stock position.

> **A collar is specifically designed as a strategy for hedging a stock position.**

While a collar can protect you from downside risk, it's not a perfect hedge. It also takes away the majority of your upside potential leaving you with a narrow band of potential outcomes. The primary purpose of a collar is protection and it comes at the expense of potential profit. That's not to say you can't make money once you apply a collar. You can make a profit, but as is the case with most hedging strategies, the upside is often very limited.

A collar is specifically designed as a strategy for hedging a stock position. For those of you who actually own stocks right now, this strategy is something you should definitely take a closer look at.

A collar is an easy way to get stock insurance. Later on, I'm going to show you how to get someone else to pay for that insurance. In a sense, this is like getting a free insurance policy on stock you own.

COLLARS—FREE INSURANCE

The foundation of the collar strategy is stock you already own that you want to protect in a bear market. The basic concept of a collar involves combining two simple conservative option strategies, first a covered call and second a protective put

To summarize:

- Use on stocks you own.
- Sell covered calls.
- Use income to buy puts.

- Insures against losses.

- Depending on stock, may still allow for upside potential.

COVERED CALLS

Let's review the covered call strategy. If you own stock, you have the right to give another investor the opportunity to buy it from you. One way to do this is by selling a call option. Once again, we're going to be selling something we do not own, just like selling stock short.

When you sell an option, you accept an obligation. In the case of a call option, the obligation is to sell 100 shares of the underlying stock, at the strike price, for each contract you sell. If you already own the stock to fulfill this potential obligation, this trade is "covered." If you do not own the stock to fulfill the potential obligation to sell stock at the strike price, the trade is said to be "naked."

Covered calls are one of the most conservative option strategies. It's an option strategy that most brokers will permit in a retirement account. A naked call, on the other hand, is one of the riskiest option strategies. Like selling stock short, the risk of a naked call is unlimited. A naked call is when you give someone the right to buy stock from you that you don't own. The option contract gives them the right to buy those shares at a set price on or before the expiration day of the option. If the stock rises above the strike price of that option, you are obligated to buy stock at the current higher price to fulfill your obligation. Since there is no limit on how high a stock may rise, the naked call has virtually unlimited risk.

When you sell a call option, you collect a premium from the buyer, although you'll never actually meet the buyer of the call options you sell. The options exchange and your brokerage firm handle the process of matching option buyers and sellers. You never have to worry about finding a buyer if you want to sell call options. You simply need to check the current bid price being offered for the call contract you want to sell and then place an order. The exchange will match your order with a buyer willing to pay you the market price for the call. The income from the call option sell is deposited into your account the next business day. It's worth mentioning, again, that option trades settle in one day; whereas stock trades normally take three days to settle.

When you sell a covered call, you are basically giving another investor the opportunity to buy your stock at the strike price of the call option on, or before, expiration day. They will normally only exercise their right to buy your stock if the price on expiration day is higher than the strike price of the call option you sold. This would basically mean that they are buying stock from you at a below market price. When they do this, it is referred to as being "called out."

> **The collar strategy can virtually eliminate the risk of owning stock. You can apply the collar strategy to any option-able stock in your portfolio and know that even a fall to zero would not wipe you out.**

Your broker will automatically sell your stock at the strike price of your call and leave the proceeds in your account. It's possible to avoid being called out by buying back the call option prior to expiration day. If the stock has risen since you sold the call, there is a chance you will have to pay a higher price to buy it back than the premium you collected when you sold it. In this case you would suffer a loss on the option transaction. However, keep in mind that if the stock has risen, the value of the shares you own will have also gone up. The rise in the value of your stock will usually offset most or all of the loss from buying back the call option. Keep this in mind as we explain the collar, because it's an easy way to get out of the obligation to sell your stock if you decide to remove the collar before expiration day.

As I mentioned before, the second part of a collar is a protective put. This is the insurance aspect of the collar strategy that provides the downside protection against a decline in the price of the stock you own.

The collar strategy can virtually eliminate the risk of owning stock. You can apply the collar strategy to any optionable stock in your portfolio and know that even a fall to zero would not wipe you out. It's a very comforting feeling if the market has you worried. You can apply a collar and go on vacation, knowing your portfolio will be intact when you return. And to think that you can set up this strategy without risking any of your own money makes it all the better. Let's take a closer look.

APPLYING THE COLLAR

The first step in applying the collar strategy is to determine which of the stocks that you own might need a collar. Any stocks that have you worried could be due for a correction, or stocks that could be sucked down by a downturn in the market, should be considered candidates. Stocks that are up-trending are not good candidates for collars. Applying a collar to an up-trending stock could result in being called out of the stock, and it might cause you to miss a significant upward move. So the collar should be considered a defensive strategy that is used to preserve your equity in bearish market conditions. It is not a strategy that will result in windfall profits, but rather one that will help to avoid catastrophic losses caused by unexpected drops in the market.

Once you determine a stock you wish to protect, you first sell one call option for each 100 shares you own. This is the covered call strategy we mentioned a moment ago. The strike price you select is normally either the at-the-money contract (the nearest strike price to the current price of the stock) or the one above it. You want to allow yourself a little margin for error if the stock should rise rather than fall. By selecting a call option for your covered call that has a strike price slightly higher than the current price of the stock, you give yourself a little upside potential. Do not sell more call options than you have shares to cover. Remember, 100 shares per contract.

The income you collect from the covered calls is what you are going to use to purchase some protective puts. Then, select your protective puts using the same

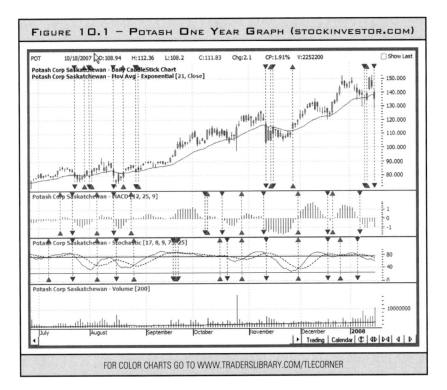

criteria we spoke about earlier in Chapter Seven. Normally you'll buy either the at-the-money contract or the next one down. This is the basic mechanics of the collar trade. I like to think of a collar as the free insurance strategy.

HOW A COLLAR WORKS

Let's look at an example using Potash (POT) stock to see how a collar works. Figure 10.1 is a graph of Potash for a one-year period. Looking at this chart it's easy to see that POT has been on a very extended run. This is the type of stock that an investor may rack up a substantial profit over this period of time that they desire to protect. That's the most common situation where a collar makes sense.

In order to consider a collar at this time, you need to consider the upside for POT to be somewhat limited in the short term. You also have to be concerned about a drop below the established support level in the $130 range. If that is your analysis, this is a perfect time to look at using a collar or a hedge.

Let's say you want to go on a vacation for two or three months, and, when you return, you want to make sure your portfolio is still intact. This is another good reason to consider applying the collar strategy. This is how it might work.

Let's take a look at the current option prices for POT options and see how we might construct a collar that protects us should the stock drop below the $130 support price. The current price of the stock is $135 and we're looking for protection to last 60 to 90 days; so we're looking at option contracts that are in March, which is 90 days from the current time frame.

POT @ $135

MAR $140 Call @ $13.70

MAR $130 Put @ $12

3 Months of Protection

$5 Deductible Before Full Coverage

$1.70 Credit ($13.70 - $12.00)

Considering the forecast for POT is limited on the upside, you want to focus on the contracts that are near, and slightly above, the current price of the stock, which is $135. This leads you to the $140 contracts. Since you are slightly optimistic on the stock, you want to give yourself a little upside potential if the stock should rally between now and March. Choosing the March 140 call option gives you almost $5 of upside potential before you put yourself in jeopardy of being called out of your stock. You collect a premium of $1370 for each call option you sell. You would consider selling one call option for each 100 shares of POT that you own. I'll show you a little twist to the collar strategy in a moment that may not require you to cover all your shares with call options, which would increase your upside potential in the collar should the stock rise. So stay tuned for that.

Options are generally quoted in "per share" increments. To figure out the cost or income for one contract, multiply the quote by 100, because there are 100 shares in each option contract. You then sell one call option for each 100 shares of CSCO stock you own.

Now you've constructed the first half of the collar. The second half is constructed by purchasing protective puts. We chose the same expiration month for the puts, as we used for the calls, to simplify the trade and to make it easier to manage.

After having determined that the support for the stock is in the $130 area, you want to look for a put that will protect you against a decline in the stock beyond that point. The nearest strike price is the $130 put. You can purchase one contract of the $130 put for $12.00 per share, or $1200 per contract.

Notice that the income you collect from selling the $140 call is $1370 and the cost of the $130 put is just $1200. This means you are able to cover the entire cost of the protective put from the proceeds of the covered call and still have a credit to your account of $170 for each 100 shares you place in the collar. If you have 500 shares of POT, you can sell 5 call contracts and buy 5 put contracts to create the collar. This gives you about $5 of upside potential in the event of a rally, but protects you against any decline in the price of the stock beyond $130. Plus, you collect $170 of excess income from the collar to minimize your downside even more.

Another option would be to construct a collar using the $135 call option rather than the $40. This would create even more income since this contract is closer to the current price of the stock, but it would limit your upside potential even more. This might be a consideration if you're very bearish about the short-term prospects of POT and wanted more downside protection. You could also adjust the strike price of the put based upon your forecast. You could lower the put strike price to cut the cost of the insurance dramatically, and thus increase the immediate income from the collar, but this would put more of the risk of an initial drop in the stock on the investor before the insurance of the put kicked in. There are many adjustments you can make in the selection of the put and call strike prices to customize the collar to match your individual forecast and objectives.

With the collar in place, we are now hedged. We can take our vacation and know that when we return, our portfolio will be intact no matter what the stock does while we're away. We don't even need to monitor the position until we return, because we know we're protected. In this example, our maximum loss—even had POT dropped to zero—would be around $12 per share.

Here's what this collar would look like if POT dropped $20 after the application of the collar.

One Week Later: POT @ $115

$20 Drop in Stock Price

MAR $130 Put @ $20.50

Loss on Stock - $20.00

Gain on Puts - $ 8.50 (20.50 – 12.00)

Collar Income - $1.70

Net Loss - $9.90 (20.00 – 8.50 (put profit) – 1.70 (collar income)

Even if POT took another steep drop, our loss on the stock would be almost completely hedged from this point forward. Here's an example of what the collar might look like if the stock dropped clear down to $90 before the collar expired.

One Month Later: POT @ $90

$45 Drop in Stock Price

MAR $130 Put @ $45.00

Loss on Stock - $45.00

Gain on Puts - $33.00

Collar Income - $1.70

Net Loss   - $10.30

On the upside, we have given ourselves $5 of an upside move before we would ever get called out. Although we have capped our upside potential by selling a covered call, we have still given ourselves room to make some additional money if the stock rises. The maximum upside potential is the strike price of the call we sell plus the income from the collar, which in this case would be $141.70 ($140 call strike price + $1.70 collar income).

This is a wonderful strategy that every investor should understand. It really is free stock insurance. Just imagine how different you might feel right now had you used the collar strategy to protect yourself against the potential of a bear market when stocks began to stall at all-time highs in late 1999 and begin to turn south in March of 2000. You could have preserved your portfolio profits at the peak of the market, and it wouldn't have cost you a dime to do it.

Now when you are too scared to stay in the market, but you don't want to sell everything, as that would trigger tax consequences, why not apply a simple collar? This is a great a way to protect your portfolio while you are waiting out a bear market.

REVIEW OF POTASH COLLAR

So let's review our Potash collar example:

- Stock currently at $135

- Put protects you from a loss below $130

- Income from call pays for put

- Allows upside to $141.70

With the stock trading at $135, we sell the $140 call and collect some income. This gives us a bit of upside potential before being put at risk of getting called out of our stock. Then, we use the income from the call options to buy the $130 put for the same expiration month. The put will protect us against any decline in the stock beyond $130. The difference between $135 current stock price and the $130 put strike price is just like our deductible on an insurance policy. That's the risk we must assume before the protection of the put kicks in. After we pay for the puts, we still have $1.70 left over, which reduces our total downside risk even more and creates some immediate income from the collar.

CLOSING OUT A COLLAR

Now let's look at how to close out a collar as expiration day nears, or when we see the stock begin to form a new uptrend. Closing it out can be done anytime before the option expires—in this case, anytime before the third Friday in April. When you remove a collar, you're basically "uncovering" your stock and closing out your insurance policy.

SELL PUTS AND BUY BACK CALLS

To get out of one of these trades, we simply just do the opposite of what we did to get into it. Remember, we sold calls and we bought puts. So to get out of the collar, we're going to buy calls and/or sell puts.

Buying back our covered calls uncovers our stock and removes the potential of getting called out of it. We must do this prior to expiration day if we don't want to run the risk of having our stock called away. Then, we sell the put options for whatever value there is and collect some money. The value of the puts will likely be very small, unless the stock has dropped since you applied the collar; so make sure you can at least collect enough to cover the cost of the commission for selling them, or simply let them expire. It's not a big deal. It's just like the insurance company getting to keep your homeowner's premium because your house didn't burn down.

That's the general concept of closing out a collar. Now let's look at the specifics based on what the stock does after you apply the collar. There are basically three things that can happen after you apply the collar: the stock can go up, down, or sideways. Let's look at each and explain how you might react.

STOCK PRICE GOES UP

If the stock rises after you create your collar, you may need to take some follow-up action based upon your forecast for the stock going forward. If the stock has risen above the strike price of your covered call, you are in jeopardy of getting called out of your shares. You need to determine if that's what you want or if you'd rather get out of this situation to keep your shares.

I'm usually one to say that if you're going to get called out, let the shares go. Too often I've seen investors buy back the call options to avoid getting called out, only to have the stock drop once they no longer have the protection the call offered. I consider getting called out to be too much of a good thing, not a bad thing.

Much like with a traditional covered call play, you've got two forces at work on the premium of the call. The natural decay of time is reducing the value of the call, while the rise in the stock is increasing it. If the stock rises substantially over the strike price of the covered call, you may be faced with the prospect of paying more to buy the call back than you collected when you sold it. This creates a loss, but you should remember that the shares of stock you own will have risen dollar for dollar with the stock and should create enough of an increase in your equity to offset the loss. It's when I'm going to take a large loss by buying back the call that I usually choose to simply let my shares get called away. With trading costs at such reasonable levels, I can always re-enter the stock position if I decide I still want to own it—and all it will cost me is another commission.

If the stock has risen, but not passed the strike price of the covered call, you do not have to worry about getting called out. The call option will expire worthless, and you'll be in a position to decide whether you want to place another collar for the next month, or perhaps just a covered call—or perhaps leave your stock uncovered completely. The choice is yours.

STOCK PRICE GOES DOWN

If the stock declines after you place a collar, it will reduce or eliminate your risk. If the stock falls and remains below the strike price of the call, the call option will usually expire worthless. The put, on the other hand, will increase in value as the stock price falls. If you selected a put with a strike price below the price of the stock, you will have to wait until you cover your deductible before the benefits of the protective put kick in. Once the stock passes the strike price of your protective put, you're insured dollar for dollar all the way to zero.

On or before expiration day, you need to decide if you'd like to exercise your put or simply sell it. Exercising the put results in your stock being sold at the strike price. If the stock has fallen since you put on the collar, this will most likely be an above-market price, and you might be very happy to sell your shares at that price and move on.

The most common thing investors in this position do is simply sell the put option and use the profit to offset the paper loss on their stock. This allows them to keep their stock and not realize any gain, or loss, on a sale for tax purposes.

STOCK PRICE STAYS THE SAME

The final scenario is if the stock doesn't go down or up, but stays right where it was when you put on the collar. In this scenario, you don't need to do anything. The covered calls can expire worthless, as can the protective puts. You have had the benefit of the insurance without any cost, and now you're in a position to decide what you want to do with your stock going forward.

If you still like the stock and feel the company has potential, you can choose to hold onto your shares. But if you no longer believe this company has promise, you are free to sell and move on. You are also in a position to apply the collar or any other strategy that allows you to extend the trade with some form of insurance or income. It's nice to have options! (Pun intended!)

The collar is a wonderful strategy. It is simple, effective, and easy to monitor. You can put a collar on for two or three months—or however long you are worried about the market—and almost forget about it. I find a collar makes me almost wish my stock would fall, so I could get the satisfaction of knowing I picked the right strategy to protect my investment. Imagine wishing your stocks would fall!

KEY POINTS TO THE COLLAR STRATEGY

SELL ENOUGH CALLS TO PAY FOR PUTS

It is important to make sure you sell enough call options to generate the cash necessary to pay for the puts. As you check the option quotes on stocks you own, you may find there are some that allow a little flexibility in how many calls you must sell to pay for the puts. The key is to make sure you're totally covered on the downside for all the shares you own. If you don't cover all your shares, it's not a problem—it could actually be a big benefit. By not covering all your shares, you have some that are not at risk of getting called away, no matter how high the stock may go. Leaving some shares uncovered allows you to have a greater upside potential on your collar. So try to sell just enough calls to pay for the puts you need to buy. Look at the protective puts you plan to buy and then figure out exactly how many calls you need to sell in order to cover their cost.

Let's say you have 1,000 shares and you decide you want to buy the protective put with the first strike below the current price of the stock. For this example, let's assume that this put is trading for $3. To purchase 10 contracts to protect your 1,000 shares will cost you $3,000. Let's say that when you look at the call options, you see that you can sell the first contract above the price of the stock and collect a premium of $5. It will only take six contracts of the call options to generate the $3,000 you need to cover the cost of the protective puts. You could sell six covered calls and leave 400 of your shares uncovered. This would allow you to profit on those 400 shares by as much as the stock happens to rise, without worrying that your stock might be called away.

USE OUT-OF-THE-MONEY OPTIONS

I like to set up my collars using out-of-the-money options. This means that I prefer to look at the call options with strike prices just above the current stock price and put options just below it. By going out-of-the-money, you'll find the options are cheaper and make it easier to get the benefits the collar provides.

USE OPTIONS THAT EXPIRE AT THE SAME TIME

It is easiest to use options that expire at the same time when you do a collar. There is no rule that says it only works if the options expire at the same time, but it will complicate your collar if the put and call expire at different times.

USE TWO- OR THREE-MONTH OPTIONS

Let's say you don't feel like you want to have your stock covered for more than a month, but you want the downside protection for two months. You could sell a call that is out just one month and buy a put that is out two. The problem with this is that it will make the options difficult to match in price. You may find that the money you collect from covering 100 percent of your shares is not enough to cover the puts you want to buy. In some circumstances that might be fine, but it does make the collar a bit more difficult to create and you may lose the added benefit of doing it without any out-of-pocket expense.

I firmly believe that every investor should learn the collar strategy if they are going to invest in a volatile market. When the market gets choppy, the collar provides an easy way to move to the sidelines, and to sit things out without selling out.

Simply put, a collar is a low-risk strategy that allows you to make a mistake and still not get hurt too badly. That makes the collar a good strategy to use in order to learn more about how options work. I hope you enjoy this new arrow in your quiver.

— — —

REVIEW

1. The strategy used by farmers to protect against dramatic changes in crop prices is known as _____.

2. A collar is a created by combining a covered call with a _____.

3. A collar is typically created by first selling the _____ call option.

4. **TRUE OR FALSE:** A collar has limited upside potential.

5. If the stock price is above the strike price of the call option you have sold on expiration day, what will happen?

FOR ANSWERS GO TO: WWW.TRADERSLIBRARY.COM/TLECORNER

CHAPTER 11

SUMMARY

As we bring things to a conclusion, I want to make sure you understand that investing in a bear market doesn't have to be harder than investing in a bull market, it's just different. If you understand the simple ways to protect yourself against losses and find opportunity as stocks fall, you'll be a better investor.

Markets don't always go up, but most investors seem to expect this outcome. When stocks begin to fall, many investors simply don't know what to do. As a result, they continue to do what they have found to be successful in a bull market, but with dramatically different results.

When you're prepared for anything, and have the tools to adapt your investing to a change in the market, the impact can be dramatic. The one or two percent you save by using a stop or a protective put could amount to thousands of more dollars in your account by the time you get to retirement age. That's the value of a financial education.

As I've traveled the world and have taught thousands of investors, I've recognized a simple fact. Nearly every investor I've met struggles when the markets are flat and down. I would say it's universally the biggest weakness of most individual investors. They don't know how to make money unless the market is going up. Good thing it goes up more than it goes down.

In athletics, if you want to improve your performance, you focus your training on your biggest weakness. It's no different with investing. Investors need to spend more time learning how to protect themselves and profit when the market dips. The money they save from doing something as simple as using a stop loss order on each trade can amount to several percent a year on their total portfolio. Compound that over their investing lifetimes and it amounts to thousands of dollars and potentially tens or even hundreds of thousands of dollars for some. Imagine that: all of that extra profit without having to pick a single different investment! Just protect the ones you make. It's the easiest and fastest way for just about every individual investor to improve their returns immediately. You just have to do it.

I thought it might be wise to summarize some of the important points I've tried to make throughout the course of this book, so that you have a good idea of where to start. The worst thing you can do at this point is nothing. So try to find one thing you've read in this book that can have a positive impact on your investing and start there. Continue to experiment and test the other strategies until you find the ones that work for you.

Hopefully, you feel more confident about investing now that you have some tools and resources to help you in either up or down markets. When the market is bearish, you need to do two things. The first is to protect your portfolio from losing money, and the second is to find ways to profit when stocks are falling.

There is always someone making money in the stock market, no matter what the market is doing. There is always an opportunity if you know where to look and how to take advantage of it. Hopefully, you've picked up on a few ways now that we've gone through this book.

> There is always someone making money in the stock market, no matter what the market is doing. There is always an opportunity if you know where to look and how to take advantage of it.

There are just a few things I want you to keep in mind. The best thing you can do now, after having read this book, is to go through each of the examples again. I have detailed them very clearly here, and, hopefully, you can look at these and follow along. Get online and start looking at some of the stocks you own or the stocks you have been watching. If you can put yourself in the mindset and apply the things we have discussed, then you will begin to feel more confident with them. Knowledge helps make you more confident in the decisions you make when your money is at stake.

DON'T LET YOUR EMOTIONS TAKE OVER

The first thing we have to learn is to control our emotions, especially the emotion of fear—the fear of losing money, the fear of making a mistake, or the fear of admitting we have made a mistake. There is also the more subtle fear of not wanting to give up a profit. All of these fears are important to know and recognize. Failure to recognize them when your emotions are impacting your investment decisions can lead to significant losses.

You should try to overcome the tendency to be an eternal optimist. The eternal optimist is usually the last one out of the market after everyone else has already run for the exit. It's not a very pleasant position. Some of you might feel like you're in that spot right now. It's vitally important for you to understand that the markets don't always go up. We have been spoiled rotten over the last few years because they have. But we've gotten a little dose of reality lately as the markets turned bearish. Take heart; this, too, shall pass.

THE TREND IS YOUR FRIEND

The next thing is to recognize that the trend is your friend. I think recognizing trends is one of the most important skills you need to acquire as an investor. I've emphasized this throughout and have given you some approaches, strategies, and resources to help you recognize the trends. Before you ever invest a penny, you should be aware of the major trends in the market, sectors, and individual stocks you are considering. When the trend is moving up, that's when you want to be invested.

Never trust technical indicators over trends. These two tools should be used in conjunction to help you make important investment decisions. Trusting indicators more than trends may result in getting caught in those bull traps of which we spoke. Stick with the indicators in the up-trending markets, and you will find a higher percentage of success in your trades.

CASH IS KING

A bull market has followed nearly every bear market in the history of the stock market. After the last major bear market in 1974, the market rose for six straight years, and eight of the next nine. The total rise in the market over that period of time was a staggering 366 percent. Since the Bear Market of 2000-2003 the market has enjoyed another 5-year bull market that has seen many stocks recover all the losses from the bear market and move to new highs. This cycle will always continue.

Fortunately, bear markets are usually over quickly and we get back to investing on the upside of the market. The key is to make sure you have some money left to invest when the market finally turns. That's why I like to say "cash is king" in a bear market. If you blow out your account in the bear market, you won't have any capital left to invest when the bargains are abundant and the market starts to rise again.

At the beginning of this book I asked you to ask yourself if you would be better off today had you earned interest on your money from 2000-2003 rather than having it invested in your portfolio? All of a sudden interest isn't looking like the same old boring investment you thought it was. There is a time to be aggressive and there are times to be conservative. The key is recognizing the difference.

LIVE TO TRADE ANOTHER DAY

The last thing is the most important. The number one rule of investing should always be "live to trade another day." I don't mean that literally, but figuratively. We don't want to risk everything we have on one bad trade. A mistake like that would make it impossible to ever recover. Money management and risk management are critical elements of any successful investing program. This really holds true when it comes to investing in a bear market. Don't be an eternal optimist riding a bad trade down to nothing. There are plenty of signals—and plenty of warning signs telling you to get out before that point.

As I look back on my individual investing experience, I see that I've learned this valuable lesson. I can remember times when it was easy to risk all my savings on one single trade in hopes of a big windfall profit. (It seems like we all like to take the biggest risks with our money when we can least afford the consequences.) Now that I'm in a position to take substantial risks and live with the consequences, I can't bring myself to the point to take them anymore. Experience is a great teacher.

I believe that a wise man learns from his mistakes, but a wiser man learns from the mistakes of others. I've made many mistakes with my own money and investments. I hope you're able to learn from some of the lessons I've learned so you can avoid the consequences of making bad decisions. If you can avoid one bad trade after reading this book, you'll have gotten a great return on your investment of time and money spent to get it.

So there you have it, a few simple tools to help you manage your investments in a volatile market. Now you can honestly say you have a simple plan to help you survive in these challenging markets. As bleak as this may get, let me assure you that there will be another nice bull market again (hopefully sooner, rather than later). It will be another great opportunity to play the upside of the market. Remember, there are always corrections along the way in the stock market. Success comes through learning now how to adjust your positions and approaches as well as handling the emotions that will always be present.

Thanks for reading. I hope it has been a great experience for you. I hope I'll have the opportunity to help you learn more about investing in one of my company's many investing programs and products. I've included some additional information about our various training programs in the back of this book.

More information is also available online at our web site, www.Stockinvestor.com. Best of luck, and we'll see you online.

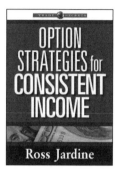

Marketplace Books is the preeminent publisher of trading, investing, and finance educational material. We produce professional books, DVDs, courses, and electronic books (ebooks) that showcase the exceptional talent working in the investment world today. Started in 1993, Marketplace Books grew out of the realization that mainstream publishers were not meeting the demand of the trading and investment community. Capitalizing on the access we had through our distribution partner Traders' Library, Marketplace Books was launched, and today publishes the top authors in the industry—household names like Jack Schwager, Oliver Velez, Larry McMillan, Sheldon Natenberg, Jim Bittman, Martin Pring, and Jeff Cooper are just the beginning. We are actively acquiring some of the brightest new minds in the industry including technician Jeff Greenblatt and programmers Jean Folger and Lee Leibfarth.

From the beginning student to the professional trader, our goal is to continually provide the highest quality resources for those who want an active role in the world of finance. Our products focus on strategic information and cutting edge research to give our readers the best education possible. We are at the forefront of digital publishing and are actively pursuing innovative ways to deliver content. At our annual Traders' Forum event, our readers get the chance to learn and mingle with our top authors in a way unprecedented in the industry. Our titles have been translated in most major world languages and can be shipped all over the globe thanks to our preferred online bookstore, TradersLibrary.com.

VISIT US TODAY AT:

WWW.MARKETPLACEBOOKS.COM & WWW.TRADERSLIBRARY.COM